DONNER PARTY COOKBOOK
A GUIDE TO SURVIVAL ON THE HASTINGS CUTOFF

Second Edition

Terry A. Del Bene

GRANDMA'S CABIN BOOKS
ENCAMPMENT, WYOMING

Donner Party Cookbook
A guide to Survival on the Hastings Cutoff

Second Edition copyright ©2015 Terry A. Del Bene

All rights reserved, including the right of reproduction in whole or any part in any form.

Del Bene, Terry Alan
Donner Party Cookbook: A guide to survival on the Hastings Cutoff

Originally published by Horse Creek Publications, Inc. ©2003

ISBN-13: 978-1-941694-02-2
ISBN-10: 1941694020

Cover illustration: Christopher R. Murray
www.chrismurrayart.com

Published by: Grandma's Cabin Books
Encampment, Wyoming

Contents

Historical Introduction	1
Culinary Introduction	9
Life on the Trail	19
Hell Freezes Over	43
Recipes	91
Gruel	92
Lumpy Dicks	93
Corn Dodgers	94
Slapjacks, Flapjacks, Pancakes, Flat Jacks	95
Johnny Cake, Journey Cake, Hoe Cake	96
Son of a Sea Dog, Hish and Hash	97
Antelope Pudding	98
Arrowroot Pudding	100
Rice Pudding	101
Brain Stew	102
Buffalo Stew	103
Mutton Soup	104
Potato Soup	105
Ox Tail Soup	106
Irish Potato Salad	108
Bacon and Rice	109
Baked Beans	110
Walnut Catsup	111
Rabbit	112
Venison	113
Scrapple	114
Mince Meat	115
Buffalo Tongue	116

Elk Roast	117
Patty Melt	118
Petite Chicken Pie	119
Grand Chicken Pie	120
Slovenly Josephs	121
Unkempt Josephs	122
Hash	123
Jerked Meat	124
Basic Bread	125
Hard Bread, Hardtack, Biscuit, Hard Crackers	126
Rice Bread	128
Corn Bread	129
Cinnamon Loaf	130
Pound Cake	131
Crumb Cake	132
Baked Apples	133
Ginger Cakes	134
Lady Fingers	135
Coffee	136
Carrot Coffee	137
Planning Your Own Donner Party	139
Bibilography	147
About the Author	152

Dedication

This book is dedicated to the men, women, and children of the Donner Party, their antagonists, their rescuers, and those who picked up the pieces of so many shattered lives. Their saga has much to say about human nature. Luis and Salvador, the only humans in the party known to be murdered specifically to provide food, deserve special recognition as being the victims of circumstances and the racism of the times. These Native American men unselfishly stayed to help strangers who were in trouble and in the end their humanity was rewarded with violence. Is this not a story as much for our century as it was for the 19th century?

Additionally I wish to dedicate this book in loving memory of my father, Howard Julius Del Bene, who taught me how to cook. He also taught me to honor the past and keep a sense of humor. I hope this book manages to package all these important life lessons in one place.

Acknowledgements

My thanks go out to all my friends involved in living history and historical interpretation. They have helped me immeasurably in improving the authenticity of my attempts at recreating 19th century cooking. My special thanks to Debra A. Varley, Kathy Gilbert, Candy Moulton, Rebecca J. Sissman, Jerry Spellman, and Chris Blasi for their constructive comments during the drafting of this book. Amanda Varley was one of the first edition's greatest promoters and contributed greatly to its success.

Georges "Buck" Damone III created the map and deserves great praise for his efforts. It is not an easy task to reconcile several historical maps into one.

Kathy Gilbert, Candy Moulton, Will Bagley, and Kristin Johnson were kind enough to go through drafts and provide editorial assistance. Without their encouragement and good suggestions, this endeavor most likely would not have happened. I accept full responsibility for any shortcomings in this document. I owe much to my friends and many anonymous donors of historical recipes that have been adapted here. Will Bagley, Kristin Johnson, Michael Landon, and the History Division of the Church of Jesus Christ of Latter-day Saints were most helpful in providing information on historical resources. Sue and Ned Schrems took a chance on publishing the first edition at Horse Creek Publications, Inc.

I especially want to thank the fine people at Grandma's Cabin for resurrecting the book and seeing it through the process of producing a revised and expanded second edition.

Preface to Second Edition

The tale of the 1846-1847 Donner-Reed Party (more commonly called the Donner Party) is one of those fascinating episodes of American history where there is a wealth of awareness but not much knowledge. Many of us learned in our childhood of the Donner Party. However, we learned almost exclusively about the cannibalism. The grisly scenes conjured up by thoughts of starving people butchering each other for food have captured the imagination. The thought of cutting up one's companions and relatives for sustenance causes one to shudder.

There is much more to the Donner Party story than cannibalism. This was a group of ordinary people caught in extraordinary circumstances, mostly of their own making. The events surrounding this group of people lead us to ponder, "What would I do if I were starving? Is preservation of one's life worth throwing away the moral codes by which we live? How far would I go to survive?" There is the hook!

Perhaps the fascination in this matter comes from our own lack of experience with what it is to be truly hungry. Most of us born after the Second World War in western industrialized countries have little concept of what it is like to be truly hungry. Though malnutrition may be found in unfortunate conditions within the United States, there have been few instances of mass starvation in living memory. For the most part, these were caused by temporary shortages of food in the general area or administrative neglect within prisons or Indian reservations. We are accustomed to believe that mass starvation is something that happens in far-off continents and in places with unfamiliar names. However, hunger and starvation are beasts that can stalk any corner of the world, even in a land of plenty.

For those who wish to find recipes for the preparation of human flesh, this book will be a disappointment. The Donner Party certainly had no recipes for the preparation of human flesh at the start of their journey. No recipes survived the ordeal. There were numerous recipes for other types of meat that could have been adapted to make their grisly feast more palatable. However, this book does not speculate on those matters. In fact, almost all of the human flesh consumed by the Donner Party was roasted over an open fire. Organs, such as brains, probably were stewed or roasted.

The intent of this book is to provide an excuse for those who have heard a little about the Donner Party to learn more about the events surrounding their rise to infamy. I have broken with academic traditions and tried to refrain from the cumbersome system of footnoting that is so common in historical works. The reader will note that most of the footnotes clarify which participants of this story are involved with each twist in the story. I want the reader to be able to read this compelling story as easily as if it were a novel. For here is a true nightmare, worthy of the pen of the best of Gothic horror writers.

Some may pick up this book out of a desire to learn. Others, no doubt, will be drawn in thinking it will provide grim humor about cannibalism. Some likely will acquire this book as a prank. Perhaps it will be a gift for a person significant in one's life — a spouse, friend, home-economics teacher, favorite chef, or parent. In occasional circumstances the book may be given in remembrance of an especially bad dinner. A few may acquire this book to learn something about cooking.

No matter what your reason for picking up this book, read on and you will find the story of people, like each of us, trying to cope with the results of decisions made on their journey through life. You might even pause before eating one of the splendid dishes presented here to remember those starving families attempting to endure the unendurable in the nightmare that passed them from just another group of travelers to the most famous wagon company to walk the trail from Missouri to California.

When the first edition of the *Donner Party Cookbook* was released it was clear that the publishing industry had difficulty trying to find its proper place in the bookstores. Is it a history? Is it a cookbook? Is it a party manual? The confusion created by the subject produced amusing moments. For a period of time the book was listed on an Atkins Diet website. Clearly the individual who made this mistake did not try the stimulating dose of carbohydrates one gets from the Lumpy Dicks recipe. Despite edition one's lack of cussing or sex and not being a how-to guide for becoming a cannibal, the book wound up being banned in particular locations, including an interpretive site dedicated to Donner Party history.

At another interpretive venue dealing with emigrant trail history, one had to whisper a request to the bookstore attendant to obtain the book as copies were discretely hidden in the storage room. An internet purveyor of books suggested that people who bought the first edition also bought *The Factor* by political pundit Bill O'Reilly and *It Takes a Village* by former First Lady/Senator/Secretary of State Hillary Clinton. Being sandwiched between those two strong and mutually hostile personalities is not a comfortable place to occupy. Since the *Donner Party Cookbook* is a non-political work, the linkage is all the more puzzling that it was not between other cookbooks and histories.

The second edition of the *Donner Party Cookbook* keeps the general formatting and "flavor" of the first edition. We have expanded the historical text and even added new recipes. Fans of the first edition often commented about including more off-color recipes such as "Frank and beans" or "Rosemary baby." For such fans it was impossible not to include a 19th century treat called ladyfingers. Since its original publication in 2003, the title of the book has been borrowed and put into print by others. Accept no substitutes, and through this second edition follow the tracks of a stubborn group of emigrants as, once mislead to a false trail, they found their land of paradise could only be entered through the gateway of a frozen hell.

Terry A. Del Bene 2015

Historical Introduction

July 19, 1846 - West of South Pass, Oregon Territory

The camp of the emigrant party was all activity that morning. Mothers gathered their children and possessions while striking the tents. Men rounded up livestock and hitched their teams, a task that had become second nature after more than a thousand miles of travel on the Oregon Trail. The oxen lowed and snorted and plumes of steamy breath billowed in the cool morning air. The dew hung heavy on equipment and the animals. The parched soil greedily absorbed the rivulets of water that rolled off the canvas as it was shaken and folded prior to being packed. The air was filled with the scent of coffee, simmering bacon grease, and the pungent smoke created by the burning buffalo chips and sagebrush used for fuel. It was time to get back on the trail.

As the wagons formed up into their usual positions, the emigrants looked around at their companions. This was the last day the entire wagon company traveled together. Some took Sublette's Cutoff to Fort Hall; others proceeded to Fort Bridger to take what was thought to be another shortcut-the newly "discovered" Hastings Cutoff.

With the opening of trails to California and Oregon, enterprising individuals, such as Lansford W. Hastings, wrote trail guides promoting their special interests in American expansion. Hastings's guide, *The Emigrants' Guide to Oregon and California,* claimed a shortcut that took travelers south of the Great Salt Lake, past the Humboldt Sink, and down the Truckee River. This was a significant deviation from what were then the most popular routes to California. It was an enticing route because Hastings claimed the shortcut saved three hundred miles, which represented about twenty-five days of travel. In truth, the cutoff was longer than trails already in use, but Hastings hoped to promote his political stock in California by bringing in emigrants along his route. There also were financial considerations such as the sale of supplies and services to emigrants, which was a growing industry. Hastings was hoping for a political and financial payoff once his route became popular.

The wagons quickly assembled in three columns to reduce the dust those at the end of the lines would have to breathe. By midday the wagon company reached the Parting-of-the-Ways where Sublette's Cutoff offered a more direct route to Fort Hall than the main trail through Fort Bridger. Here the party divided into two groups. For the most part, it was with sadness that the emigrants parted ways with their companions of many months. Together they had come more than a thousand miles. The company divided and the last good-byes were said. As they took their different paths, members of each party turned to look and get one last glimpse of their former companions. All kept on toward their goals. Some walked toward new homes and quiet lives of obscurity; others walked into a hellish ordeal and the pages of history.

Historical Perspective

Why did so many people in the 19th century decide to abandon hearth and home, load up the prairie schooner, and head west? There is no easy answer to this question. It was the lure of riches, the promise of free land, and sometimes a desire for religious freedom. Some chose to escape the crowded East, to find adventure, to maintain family ties, and a host of other reasons. Within the space of a few decades, hundreds of thousands of Americans and Europeans left their familiar worlds and set off into a new world and a new life in the American West.

By 1843, with the opening of a system of westward wagon trails, a steady flow of emigrants[1] dared the passage across the Plains in their search for paradise. They faced thousands of miles of walking. The environments they experienced on the Plains and in the Rocky Mountains were foreign to them. Disease,

---

1 Technically, the foreigners entering California should be considered immigrants. This text follows the convention of the time and refers to all the travelers as emigrants.

accidents, and violent death were the price many paid to follow their chosen dreams. Roughly one out of ten westward-bound emigrants found a final resting place on the journey. By the time the railroads and wagon road systems closed down the Oregon and California Trails, there was an average of ten emigrant graves every mile along the two thousand-plus miles of trail.

Clearly the move to a new life was not something to be taken lightly; but many Americans believed in John O. Sullivan's ideal that it was America's destiny to conquer the North American continent. The newspaper editor coined the phrase "Manifest Destiny" in 1845 to justify America's quest for new territory. The emigrants of 1846 were players in a contest for territorial expansion, and beautiful California was part of the prize. Vast expanses of fertile land, forests, mountains, and fisheries awaited the bold emigrants who made the trip from all points of the world to help tame this portion of Mexico.

In 1846 emigrants who entered the Mexican province of California were headed into the vortex of war. In April of that year, the United States and Mexico had just begun a conflict that ultimately resulted in the annexation of the American Southwest to the United States. In mid-1846 the outcome of these events was uncertain and did not bode well for Americans entering Mexican territory seeking a new life in paradise.

Already Mexico had significant trouble with American immigrants in the Mexican province of Texas. There, Americans had taken over a Mexican province and waged war against the government. Those same immigrants arranged to have the rebellious province annexed by the United States. This was intolerable to the Mexican government and it should surprise few that it was the catalyst for war. In such circumstances, many California emigrants wondered what kind of reception waited for them in California. War, however, did not stem the flow of westward-bound emigrants. Despite their concerns, many chose to travel the western trail.

Overland emigration was expensive, and the average emigrant tended to be well-to-do by 19th century standards. Many poor people completed the journey as hired help or even in migrations subsidized by the Mormon Church, the United

States government, or others. The average emigrant started on the trail fairly well supplied for the journey and for establishing a new life at the destination. Starvation, though a consideration, did not loom large as a likely outcome of travel on the trails. After all, early explorers had reported that the American West had an abundance of game and plants to sustain life.

A wagon train was its own society. Those who signed on became part of a group of people who shared the many common life experiences that ran the gamut from the celebration of holidays to the education of children. Young people met and fell in love; some married. Men and women mourned the loss of spouses; the elderly sometimes finished out their long lives on windswept plains.

A wagon train was also a microcosm of the greater Victorian society of the mid-nineteenth century. Each train had its own social structure reflecting the Victorian culture in which they lived. At the top of the social order were the wealthy, the born leaders. At the bottom were the foreign born emigrants and the lower classes. Class distinctions often were defined by the Victorians based upon country of origin, religion, language, and race. In spite of this caste system, members of each train typically worked together to overcome obstacles along the trail. In fact, some trains formed independent democracies where members voted on how to resolve issues between emigrants and how to operate the train. On some trains, however, families or individuals just didn't get along or had different interests. It was common for trains to splinter and coalesce based upon the inabilities or abilities of the emigrants to get along with their fellows.

The Donner-Reed Party followed the typical norms of the dominant Victorian culture. Both leaders, Donner and Reed, were wealthy individuals to whom the rest of the membership deferred. But uncommon hardships, bad decisions by the leaders, and the particular makeup of the people on the Donner Party train eventually caused reasonable people to throw cultural conventions to the wind for the sake of self-interest and a general lack of concern for the greater good of the whole party.

From its inception in what is now Wyoming, on July 20, 1846, the leaders of the Donner-Reed Party made fateful decisions that prevented the wagon train from successfully completing its journey to California that year. This was especially true when the leaders decided to put their trust and fate in the hands of Lansford W. Hastings and the advice offered in his guidebook, *The Emigrants' Guide to Oregon and California*. The problem with Hastings's advice was that he never attempted to traverse the route in a wagon or even on horseback until a year after his travel guide was published. Even the party that Hastings led in person, sometimes called the Harlan-Young Party, had a very rough crossing. The Donner-Reed Party followed in the faint tracks of the Harlan-Young wagons.

The route was a fraud and ultimately led many of the Donner-Reed Party to pay an extreme price. George Donner may have kept a copy of Hastings' trail guide on the journey. There is speculation that James Reed read the work prior to setting out. There is little mention, however, of consulting this guide during the journey. It was Hastings's written and personal offer to guide the emigrants that apparently convinced members of the Donner-Reed Party to follow the newest shortcut to California.

What follows is a brief history of the Donner-Reed Party and its fateful trip from Independence, Missouri, to Sutter's Fort in California. In order to keep a period feel to this history, this book presents quotations from Donner-Reed Party survivors and others associated with the story. Some of these recollections were published many years after the events of 1846-47. The precious diary of Patrick Breen is an account that was written while events were occurring. Nineteenth century writing was quite informal by our standards. There was little adherence to rules of punctuation, capitalization, and spelling. Breaks in sentences often were indicated by simply leaving additional blank spaces. The best advice to the reader is to sound out the sentences. The words were written much as they were spoken.

Despite the fact that there were many survivors and witnesses to events in the rescue parties, there remain many questions regarding specific historical points of the Donner-Reed Party. It is not our intention to wade into these controversies with new readings of the data. The focus of this tale is how a series of bad decisions made extraordinary survival techniques necessary.

What to Bring on the Trip

Preparation for a long journey on the emigrant trail system was critical. There was an abundance of advice to the prospective travelers. William B. Ide wrote the following packing list in Springfield Illinois' *Sangamo Journal*, published on September 4, 1845.

> "One waggon for four to six persons- team as above. Stout young cows preferable to oxen; horses are of little service, except to collect cattle of morning. They need to be exchanged once in seven or eight hundred mires for others if much used. One hundred pounds of hard biscuit: 150 pounds of flour: 20 pounds lard, 50 pounds com-meal, sifted, 75 pounds bacon: 5 pounds coffee, 10 pounds sugar; 1 peck beans: 50 pounds dried fruit: 5 pounds of salt: one half pound pepper: 7 pounds hard soap; 2 pounds salaratus; one half pound of spice: one half pound of cinnamon: 2 pounds ginger, a little castor oil: a little rhubarb; peppermint, camphor, and some other things such a dry body needs, but rarely think of beforehand, to each full grown person. Fifteen pounds of tar and two pounds of rosin to each waggon, 65 feet of ¾ inch rope, one set of spare shoes to each work; ox or cow, and nails, one years clothing: tarpolin hat: one water proof cloak: one rifle 32 balls to the pound: 4 pounds of powder: ten pounds of lead: one thousand percussion caps: one belt, butcher knife, scabbard, shot pouch and powder horn: one canteen or tin cup, and two Whips to each man: five pounds of salt to each head of cattle. One axe, three augers, one drawing knife, and two chisels, to each family, and one tent made of stout Osnaburg."

In his 1845 trail guide Lansford W. Hastings recommended that emigrants pack the following:

> "In treating of the equipment, supplies, and the method of traveling, I share confine my remarks, entirely, to the over land route, which lies through the great southern pass; as the chief emigration, to those countries, is, at this time, by that route, which from present indications, is

destined to become the great thoroughfare, between the States, and both Oregon and California. All persons, designing to travel by this route, should, invariably, equip themselves with a good gun; at least, five pounds of powder, and twenty pounds of lead; in addition to which, it might be advisable, also, for each to provide himself with a holster or good pistols, which would, always, be found of great service, yet they are not indispensable. If pistols are taken, an additional supply of ammunition should, also, be taken; for, it almost necessarily follows, that the more firearms you have, the more ammunition you will require, whether assailed by Indians, or assailing the buffalo. If you come in contact with the latter, you will find the pistols of the greatest importance; for you may gallop your horse, side by side, with them, and having pistols, you may shoot them down at your pleasure; but should you come in mortal conflict with the former the rifle will be found to be much more effective and terrific; the very presence of which, always, affords ample security. Being provided with arms and ammunition, as above suggested, the emigrant may consider himself, as far as his equipment is concerned, prepared, for any warlike: emergency, especially, if nature has, also, equipped him with requisite energy and courage.

In procuring supplies for this journey, the emigrant should provide himself with, at least, two hundred pounds of flour or meal, one hundred and fifty pounds of bacon; ten pounds of coffee; twenty pounds of sugar; and ten pounds of salt, with such other provisions as he may prefer, and can conveniently; take; yet the provisions, above enumerated, are considered ample, both as to quantity, and variety. It would, perhaps, be advisable for emigrants, not to encumber themselves with any other, than those just enumerated; as it is impracticable for them, to take all the luxuries, to which they have been accustomed; and as it is found, by experience, that, when upon this kind of expedition, they are not desired, even by the most devoted epicurean."

Since it was impossible to bring everything, great care was taken to include those things necessary to live.

Culinary Introduction

In his book, *The Emigrants' Guide to Oregon and California*, Lansford Hastings provided the following advice on what to bring on the long journey:

> "Very few cooking utensils, should be taken, as they very much increase the load, to avoid which is always a consideration of paramount importance, A baking kettle, frying pan, tea pot, and coffee pot are all the furniture of this kind, that is essential, which together with tin plates, tin cups, ordinary knives, forks, spoons, and a coffee mill should constitute the entire kitchen apparatus."

The following recipes are basic recipes of the time with which members of the Donner Party probably were familiar. None of the members had any recipes for human flesh before starting their journey. Perhaps Louis Keseberg had some after the journey; but despite having a brief career as a restaurateur, he apparently did not commit any to paper.

> "Bread has been the principal article of food in our camp. We laid 150 pounds of flour and 75 pounds of meat for each individual, and I fear bread will be scarce. Meat is abundant. Rice and beans are good articles on the road; cornmeal, too is acceptable." (Tamsen Donner writing on June 16, 1846)

Most of the human flesh probably was eaten roasted without seasoning. Many Donner Party survivors had difficulty admitting that they had to eat human flesh to survive much less provide a cooking guide as to how to best prepare this most unusual repast. As you will see, by modern standards 19th century cooking does not seem very healthy. The diet contained significant amounts of lard, salt, animal fats, and REAL BUTTER. When you worked as hard as our forbearers, a high-fat, high-salt diet was not a big issue. When traveling the Donner Party did at least twelve miles of walking a day plus tending the livestock, gathering fuel and water, setting up camp, breaking camp, repairing items, cooking, and hitching up the livestock each day. Imagine having to spend your day doing these things or on "tough days" cutting a road through the woods or even hauling the wagons up a sheer slope with block and tackle. For those conscious of their health who wish to try these recipes, I will leave it up to you to find substitutes or cut down on the quantities.

The 19th century kitchen contained many spices and edibles with which we present-day cooks are not familiar. I have attempted to focus upon the modern substitutes. For example, the following recipes use baking soda to assist baked goods in rising rather than the pearl ash (potassium carbonate) or saleratus (potassium bicarbonate) that would have been used by most cooks. The huge deposits of natural soda ash in the West occasionally may have provided baking soda to the emigrants identical to that which is now popular.

Even some of the most common elements of the modern kitchen are all but unrecognizable in their 19th century forms. Take, for example, sugar; in the 19th century, some sugar came in cone-shaped packages called hats or loaves. The cone was wrapped in paper dyed with indigo. The indigo discouraged hungry rodents from eating the sugar. The sugar was so hard that a special tool called "sugar nippers," which are somewhat like tongs combined with cutting pliers, was needed to break down the hat to required amounts. Modern, refined sugar seems noticeably sweeter, but the old sugar has a lighter flavor, which gives it special qualities. One may get some of this flavor back by buying natural sugar or using brown sugar. Though our ancestors had a variety of sugar products to choose from, the overall diet of the period tended to have less sugar than modern people use. If you have doubts about trying the cuisine, consult your doctor.

> *"Wood is now very scarce, but "buffalo chips" are excellent; they kindle quickly and retain heat suprisingly. We had this morning buffalo steaks broiled upon them that had the same flavor they would upon hickory coals."*
> *(Tamsen Donner letter of June 16, 1846)*

There's little mystery to cooking with buffalo chips. Collect a large pile of dried chips from the prairie. This is fairly simple in certain areas. The chips require a small fire from wood shavings, paper, bark, grease, or some other source to ignite them. Buffalo chips burn much like charcoal but with a little more smoke. There is very little flame but sufficient heat to do the cooking. It takes a large amount of chips to do anything ambitious, such as baking.

For twenty-first century people, it might be difficult to envision the skill it really took to be competent with campfire cooking and baking. Today we still barbecue extensively, but even that has become a high-tech enterprise. With the right camp gear, the average cook turned out the complete range of main dishes, baked goods, confections, and side dishes that we make in our modern kitchens. It took skill to regulate temperatures, especially if your source of heat was a smoldering pile of buffalo chips or wood coals. Cooking back then was an art and not the technical exercise it has become. When attempting the following recipes, let your inner artist come out. Sometimes allowing a few ashes from a cedar wood fire to get into the pot adds flavor.

There are few hard and fast rules in this art. Everyone needs to learn for himself the characteristic sights, sounds, smells, and tastes of success and failure. Remember, one often learns more from failure than from success. Many modern cooks have trouble adapting to food preparation that needs to be attended very closely. If one is doing the cooking well, there will be little time for anything else.

Outdoor cooks must adapt to a variety of situations created by wind, temperature, and precipitation. In many parts of the Great Western Desert, prevailing summer winds complicate the control of open campfires. A smoky fire can be a genuine tribulation when attempting to cook a meal. A dust storm is likely to make any open fire impossible. Cooking during a rainstorm can be accomplished under a canvas shelter but there could be a significant fire risk until the fabric is soaked. If a heavy rain hits and starts to flood the fire pit, one can place coals in a tin plate or pot and cook over those.

The out-of-doors cook needs to learn that it is more desirable to cook over hot coals than a fire. This lesson had to be learned by emigrants as well. Cooking over the open fire was much more tricky than cooking with a wood stove. Some emigrants actually packed wood stoves with them, only to discard them on the trail as the road became more difficult. Each emigrant family had to learn for itself the different heating qualities of each fuel source. Cedar burns differently than oak. Sage burns differently than buffalo chips. Smoky materials might add flavor to roasting meats but can make intensive tending of omelets or soups difficult.

There are numerous tricks to regulating temperature. If the fire is too cool, additional coals or hotter-burning fuels can be added to raise temperature. If the fire is too hot (the more common problem), one can reduce heat by adding water to the coals (gradually) or partially covering the coals with earth. One can also reduce heat by raising the cooking vessel higher above the coals. This could be done using stones, grates, or various adjustable contraptions, such as a tripod or "spider."

It is important to remember that baking with coals involves placing the coals over the top of the baking vessel, presumably a Dutch oven or covered pan, as well as having coals underneath. It often is easier to do the baking a few feet away from the campfire. To do this, find a bare spot of ground (or clear one) and spread out a thin layer of hot coals. Then set the cooking vessel upon these; then place an additional layer of coals on top of the cooking vessel. This little trick reduces the risk of burning your food. However, one must be very careful to make sure this is only done where the risks of starting a brushfire or prairie fire are minimal. Such a trick allowed emigrant cooks to roast food in the fire pit at high temperatures and bake dishes at lower temperatures at the same time.

Cooking in cold weather presents different challenges. Fuels tend not to perform the same in the initial stages. Once a good fire is going, though, things operate much as in warmer times; but often cooking times increase. Melting snow can extinguish the fire. Building the fire on a wooden pallet or metal sheet can reduce this problem. Cooking on a deep snow pack creates more difficulties than melting snow as the fire rapidly begins to work its way toward the ground. The fire can melt its way several feet below the level of the cook and make access to the hot coals almost impossible. As the Donner Party learned, there are ways to suspend the fire above the snow by building platforms.

Food spoilage was a problem in the mid-nineteenth century. The emigrants lacked refrigerators, plastic wrap, and many of the wondrous preservatives we take for granted. However, they were able to keep items such as butter fresh for more than a year. This involved soaking the butter in brine (often of salt, sugar, and saltpeter) and then placing it in a salted cloth covering. Eggs could be preserved for months by dipping them in a solution of borax and warm water. The emigrants canned fruits and vegetables. Fruits could be dried and rolled, too. Meats and fish can be salted, smoked, dried, or canned. A popular method to "preserve" meat was to have slaughter animals accompany the train for use along the way. Cows also provided fresh milk and chickens furnished eggs.

Nature provided animals for hunting *en route*. The emigrants hunted buffalo, bear, elk, deer, antelope, rabbit, prairie chickens, geese, ducks, hawks, eagles, and a variety of other animals available when time could be taken to go after them. There also were berries, fruits, tubers, and nuts available along the trail. Even with this host of techniques available, sometimes food spoiled. Many period recipes include spoiled food ... such that little was wasted. Even sour milk and wormy biscuits can be made edible. The truly hungry person finds a wider range of foods palatable than does a well-fed individual.

> *"Antelope and buffalo steaks were the main article on our bill of fare for weeks, and no tonic was needed to give zest for the food; our appetites were a marvel. Eliza soon discovered that cooking over a camp fire was far different from cooking on a stove or range, but all hands assisted her."* (Virginia Reed Murphy writing in 1891)

Another difficulty that our emigrant cooks had to overcome was the effect of altitude upon cooking. At high altitudes water boils at a lower temperature and the effectiveness of baking soda is reduced. A perfect bread recipe for Independence, Missouri, might not come out so well when camping at Independence Rock in modern day Wyoming, at an altitude over five thousand feet.

Nineteenth century cooks used a goodly amount of milk, including spoiled and scalded milk, in cooking all manner of dishes. We now use water in a similar fashion. Several of the recipes provide options of using milk or water. In those cases, the first liquid listed is preferred, but the second may be used.

These are not exact recipes that were necessarily used by the Donner Party, but are typical of those popular at the time. They are intended to give the reader a flavor for mid-nineteenth century cooking. If the recipes do not please the palate, then the dishes can be brought to 21st century standards perhaps by deep frying, covering with melted cheese, and capping the whole with strips of bacon.

Emigrants likely ate smaller portions than modern people enjoy. Nineteenth century dishes tend to be calorie-rich and, as such, are quite filling. It is estimated that if one were to consume modest portions of 19th century cuisine that the normal daily intake would be roughly 2,000 to 3,000 calories. For people as active and exposed to the elements as the emigrants, higher calorie counts were essential to function. For our less-active culture, filled with scientific labor saving devices, the diet would be a recipe for health problems.

> *"But it is a fact (though I think not generally known) that some people cannot subsist on meat alone, while others did not suffer at all as long as our meat lasted, but it gave out about the fifth of February, and then we had nothing but the hides of our cattle, till relief came."*
> (William C. Graves writing in 1877)

May 12, 1846 — Independence, Missouri

The great gathering place for overland emigrants was Missouri, where strangers threw in their lots together to share the great adventure ahead. The jump from "civilization" into the vast, open wilderness of the Great Western Desert took no small amount of courage. Tent cities sprang up as the emigrants came together and selected their companions for the journey. The timing of the departure was the first important decision of the trip. The emigrants needed to wait until the grasses had matured sufficiently to support their livestock. Leaving too early would mean too little grass for the livestock during the early part of the trip and high spring water at many river crossings. Too late a departure raised the specter of winter in the Sierra Nevada Mountains on the doorstep of California.

Despite the dangers and trials that loomed in front of them, the gathering or jumping off areas tended to be characterized by a sense of optimism; and such enthusiasm ran high in the camps of the Donner and James Reed families on May 12, 1846, as they hurried westward out of Independence. Their immediate goal was to join with Colonel William H. Russell's company, which had set out earlier.

James Frazier Reed[2], an immigrant to America, was forty-five years old. He was born in Ireland and eventually settled in Springfield, Illinois. There he prospered as a cabinetmaker. Reed took with him his wife of twelve years, Margaret (formerly Keyes), his mother-in-law Sarah Keyes, and four children; Virginia, Martha [Patty], James Jr., and Thomas. The Reed family was supplemented by hired helpers, Milt Elliot, Walter Herron, James Smith, Bayliss Williams, and Eliza Williams. Reed apparently was a local leader and was instrumental in organizing the first emigrating party from Springfield, Illinois.

The Reeds were a wealthy family. They could afford hired help to ease the effort of handling all the baggage and livestock. Delicacies as well as equipment and necessities of all kinds were packed within the three wagons.

One of the wagons, referred to as the "Prairie Palace," is reputed to have been larger than other wagons and to have contained bunks for sleeping. The size and appearance of the wagon are a matter of speculation. One expects diarists who saw the Reed wagons to note a larger than normal vehicle. None did. The suggestion here is that the "Prairie Palace," if it did exist, probably was a wagon within the normal size range. On the inside it might have been equipped differently than the austere interiors of most wagons.

---

2 Reed is a shortening of Reednovski. It was common practice for immigrants to America to Anglicize foreign-sounding names.

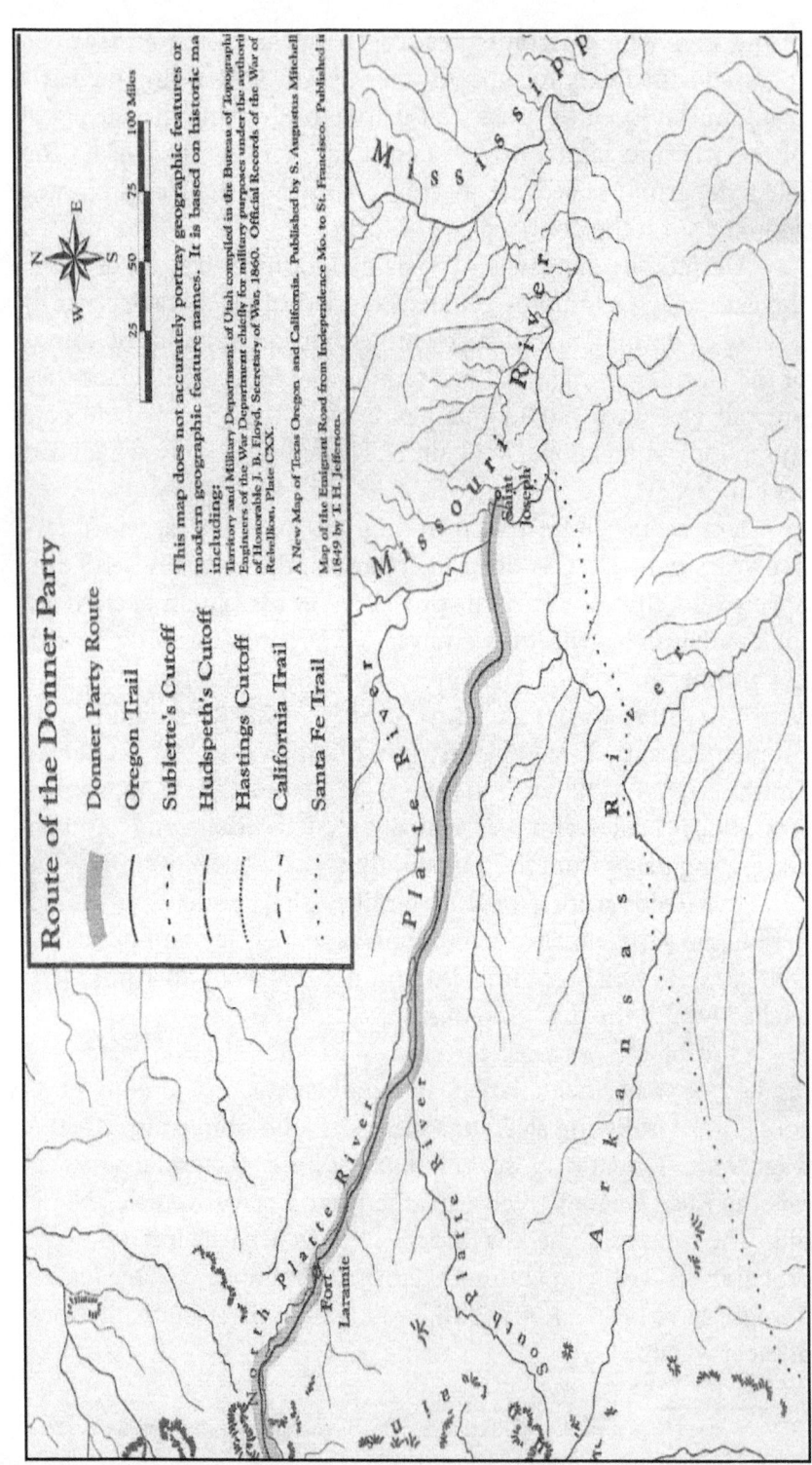

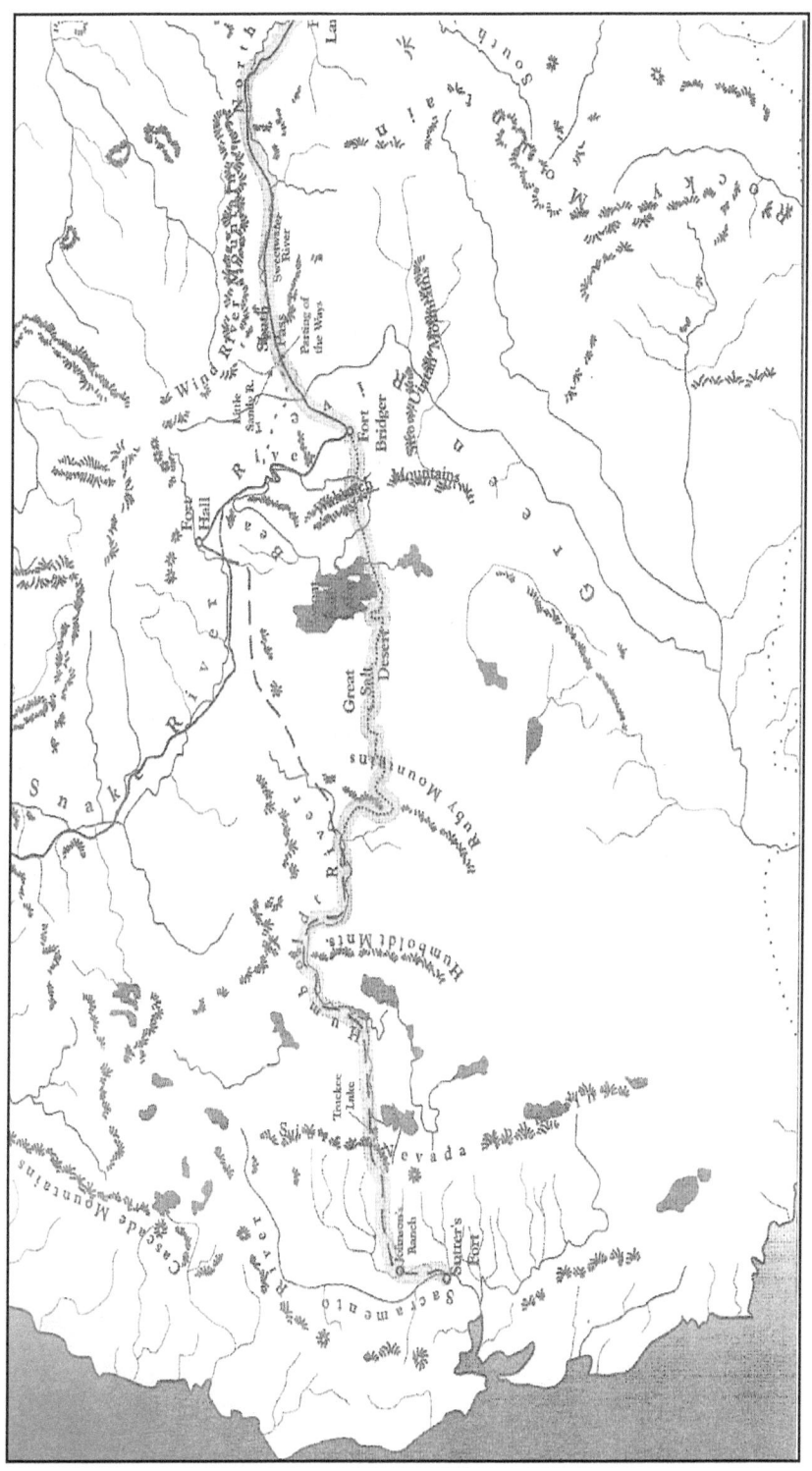

Though the road ahead contained broad desert basins and rugged mountains the Donner Party approached their journey with a sense of optimism.

Life on the Trail

Fellow Springfield residents the Jacob and George Donner families joined with the Reeds. The Donner brothers brought their wives and a total of twelve children. Jacob Donner's family consisted of his wife Elizabeth and seven children-George Jr., Lewis, Samuel, Mary, Isaac, William Hook, and Solomon Hook.[3] George Donner's family included his wife, Tamsen, and five children Frances, Elitha, Leanna, Georgia, and Eliza. John Denton, Antonio, Noah James, Hiram Miller, and Samuel Shoemaker accompanied the Donners.

Roughly one hundred miles west of Independence, the Donners and Reeds caught up with the Russell Party who were camped at Indian Creek. On May 19th, by unanimous vote, the Donner and Reed families became members of the Russell Party.[4] Edwin Bryant remarks that he thought the new additions were *"respectable and intelligent gentlemen, with interesting families."* The Russell Party now counted forty-six wagons. There were about ninety-eight men, fifty women, and numerous children in the group. Together the emigrants boasted a herd of approximately 350 cattle.

As with most wagon companies, the pace of travel was slow and measured, roughly twelve to fifteen miles a day. The company quickly developed a routine. Harnessing the oxen and caring for the family while on the move soon became second nature. Learning to cook on an open fire using wood, brush, or even buffalo droppings soon passed from a novelty to a boring reality. Even at this modest pace of travel, the work was grueling. The weak, the elderly, and the children suffered increased death rates.

---

3   William and Solomon were children of Elizabeth's from a previous marriage. Jacob Donner's son, George Jr. might be more properly referred to as George II.

4   The individuals who became the historical "Donner Party" traveled roughly half the journey from Missouri as members of the "Russell Party."

The first to die was Sarah Keyes, the mother of Margaret Reed. Sarah had been told by her doctors that she would not survive the trip. However, she wished to expend the last of her earthly efforts attempting to reach her son, who was thought to be headed east on the main California Trail. The family hoped to meet him near Fort Hall in present-day Idaho.[5] Sarah died on May 29, 1846, at the age of 70. She had not survived even three weeks of travel. Edwin Bryant, a member of the Russell Party, described the funeral:

> "At 2 o'clock, P.M., a funeral procession was formed, in which nearly every man, woman and child of the company united, and the corpse of the deceased lady was conveyed to its last resting place, in this desolate but beautiful wilderness. Her coffin was lowered into the grave .... A funeral discourse was then pronounced by the officiating clergyman, and the services concluded by another hymn and benediction. The grave was then closed and carefully sodded with the green turf of the prairie, from whence will spring and bloom its brilliant and many-colored flowers."

Some might have taken her death as a bad omen and returned to their old homes, but the Reeds, like so many others, buried their dead and continued walking westward.

The majority of the trip prior to reaching the Rocky Mountains was unremarkable and fairly typical of all wagon journeys of the period. The emigrants awakened early and started out as soon as practicable. There was an extended break at noon, called the "nooning," after which travel resumed until almost dusk or at a stopping point near a convenient campground or watering hole. Occasionally each train stopped for extended periods to rest, refit, heal the sick and injured, and bring in supplies.

The party moved west one step at a time. Few were the emigrants who rode in the wagons. The average wagon was packed with food, supplies, tools, and furniture. All were needed for the trip or eventually setting up a new life at the trip's destination. The sick and infirm were allowed to ride, but the experience was not

---

[5] If this is correct, it is compelling evidence that the Reeds did not intend to follow the Hastings Cutoff at the start of their journey as that route does not pass through Fort Hall.

a restful one. The wagons lacked sophisticated shock absorbers, if they had any at all. This made for a most uncomfortable ride. Each bump of the uneven trail could become a bone-jarring blow administered by the wagon to the unfortunate passenger despite the best attempts at padding.

The inclusion of fresh game in the diet was critical to a successful crossing. This supplemental sustenance allowed the emigrants to carry more than just the food necessary for the journey. It allowed them to save butchering of cattle for later in the trip, and sometimes allowed trains to get all the way to California with a herd of cattle that was almost intact. A disruption in the game herds could make for a tough crossing forcing the emigrants to slaughter livestock to survive. However, in mid-June it appeared that the members of the wagon train were likely to have a safe and fairly uneventful crossing and were anticipated to arrive in California with their population of domesticated animals mainly intact.

June 27, 1846 — Fort Laramie, Oregon Territory

Near the end of June, the Russell Party arrived at fabled Fort Laramie, in present-day eastern Wyoming. Here they were able to have equipment repaired and even purchase delicacies at the trading post. The emigrants probably wished to linger at Fort Laramie, but their stay was short and they celebrated the Fourth of July some miles west of Fort Laramie. The Russell Party's celebration included soothing lemonade and more. According to Edwin Bryant, James Reed had kept aside fine wines and liquors for the national birthday. As was typical of the time, the celebration consisted of speeches, a reading of the Declaration of Independence, gunfire, dancing, fiddling, and a fair amount of drinking.

> "On the Platte we stayed a week, laying in a stock of buffalo meat. We encamped about two miles from a buffalo lick, to which thousands of those animals came to lick the salt with which the earth was impregnated. July 4 found us filled with Buffalo meat and patriotism, and after our usual dance, we youngsters drew up in line to fire a salute, which was done without other loss of killed

or wounded than a young fellow named Bill Richardson, who, in order to make greater noise, had overloaded his Yager rifle and got knocked a rod or so out of line, his rifle flying forty feet away." (Jacob W. Harlan writing in 1888)

It was near Fort Laramie that they met eastbound members of the Clyman-Hastings-Hudspeth Party. That group had been the first to follow the Hastings Cutoff. They had traveled from west to east on the route that eventually brought disaster to the Donner Party. In 1845 Lansford W. Hastings, in his *The Emigrants' Guide to Oregon and California,* presented a "quick and easy" route to California. He promoted a "short cut" which, though not explicitly described, would take emigrant wagons off the main Oregon Trail near Fort Bridger, south of the Great Salt Lake, across the Great Salt Desert, through the Ruby Mountains, and then link back to the California Trail. Much of this was a significant deviation from what were then the most popular routes to California. Hastings hoped to promote his political stock in California by bringing in emigrants on his shortcut. He also had financial interests; selling supplies and services to emigrants was a growing industry.

Hastings claimed that his cutoff reduced the journey to California by 300 to 400 miles.[6] If true, the cutoff saved roughly a month in travel time. According to Hastings, the route was good for wagons and the only difficult pull would be in the vicinity of the Great Salt Lake, where a short stretch lacked water. To emigrants in a hurry to start their new lives, the route seemed to offer many advantages.

When the party met up with him near Fort Laramie, James Clyman, the famed mountain man, was reputed to have strongly warned the Russell Party, however, that the Hastings Cutoff was not practical for wagons. Clyman and James F. Reed had served in the same unit during the Blackhawk War[7] and are thought to have had an extensive talk about the safest route.

---

6   The Hastings cutoff actually increased the mileage. Unfortunately Hastings had not traveled his shortcut until a year after publishing his travel guide. Even after his rough easterly trip along the route in 1846, Hastings had no evidence that his route was shorter than the main emigrant trails already in common use. However, he stuck to his fraudulent selling point and convinced many to follow him on the new route.

7   Clyman and Reed served in the same unit as future President of the United States, Abraham Lincoln.

In the aftermath of the Donner Party's disastrous journey, Clyman related, "I told him to take the regular wagon track and never leave it—it is barely possible to get through if you follow it, and it may be impossible if you don't." Clyman's diary reference about the meeting does not mention Reed by name but mentions carrying on a conversation "until a late hour" with California-bound emigrants. Clyman suggested that his talk changed the destinations of several emigrants from California to Oregon. Clyman's account is sketchy, however. It appears that he had his first cup of coffee here in many months and the enjoyment of that simple pleasure made more of an impression on him at the time than his role in the fate of one of the most famous emigrant parties in history. Of course, Reed and the members of the Russell party that were to form the Donner Party weren't famous yet when Clyman met them near Fort Laramie.

On July 11th the emigrants were camped near Independence Rock when they received a letter, carried by Wales Bonney, from Hastings. The open letter indicated that it would be in the best interests of the emigrants to band together and take his new shortcut. Hastings created a story that the California government was raising an army to keep Americans out. This fictional threat, together with the promised ease and shorter length of the route, was very persuasive. Many in the party ignored Clyman's warning. James Reed was in a hurry and believed Lansford Hastings's claims that this new route reduced the trip by roughly three hundred miles over the more commonly used Fort Hall route. He offered to lead those who would follow along the supposedly shorter Hastings Cutoff. In fact, the Hastings Cutoff would add weeks to the journey.[8]

---

8   According to G.R. Stewart (The California Trail, Lincoln, University of Nebraska Press, 1962), the distances between the Parting-of-the-Ways and the point where the Hastings Cutoff reunites with the California Trail are as follows for the three options available to emigrants in 1846; Fort Bridger Route- 585 miles, Sublette Cutoff- 500 miles, Hastings Cutoff- 595 miles. Accordingly Hastings' "shortcut" was anywhere from 10 to 95 miles longer than the other routes. The difficult terrain of the Hastings Cutoff cost travelers additional time over that required to traverse the main routes in use in 1846. Time was a most valuable commodity.

> "My father was so eager to reach California that he was quick to take advantage of any means to shorten the distance, and we were assured by Hastings and his party that the only bad part was the forty mile drive through the desert by the shore of the lake. None of our party knew then, as we learned afterwards, that these men had an interest in the road, being employed by Hastings. But for the advice of these parties we should have continued on the old Fort Hall road." *(Virginia Reed Murphy in 1891)*

July 19, 1846 — Parting-of-the-Ways

On July 19, 1846 the Russell Company came to the Parting-of-the-Ways, just west of South Pass, where the trail crossed the Continental Divide. At the Parting-of-the-Ways the trail forked into two branches. One branch followed the original Oregon Trail southwest to Fort Bridger and then northwest to Fort Hall. The other fork followed Sublette's Cutoff, which headed more or less directly west, thus eliminating the need to go first south and then back north and providing a shortcut to get from the Parting to Fort Hall.

The advent of the Hastings Cutoff provided a third alternative. It also took off from Fort Bridger but headed more or less directly west from there rather than northwest to Fort Hall. From the Russell wagon train, seventy-one people decided to turn southwest toward Fort Bridger and, from there to follow the Hastings Cutoff. For the most part, the divisions were made along family lines. The Bridger-bound party included the Reed, Donner, Murphy, Breen, Keseberg, Wolfinger, and Eddy families and their traveling companions.[9] It is here that Hiram Miller left his fellow Springfield residents and went ahead with the Bryant-Russell pack train.

---

9   The Breen family included Patrick, Margaret, John, Edward, Patrick Jr., Simon, James, Peter, and Isabella. The Breens were accompanied by Patrick Dolan. The Eddy family included William, Eleanor, Margaret, and James. The Murphy family included John, Levinah (a.k.a. Lavinia), Mary, Lemuel, William, and Simon. Associated with them were William Pike, Harriet Pike, Naomi Pike, Catherine Pike, William Foster, Sarah Foster, and George Foster. The Keseberg family included Louis, Phillipine, Ada, and Louis Jr. The Wolfinger family included Jacob and Dorothea. Additionally these groups were joined by Charles Stanton, James Smith, Joseph Reinhard, Walter Herron, and Mr. Hardcoop. The party added Luke Halloran at the Little Sandy River, a few miles west of Parting-of-the-Ways.

Nineteen wagons and stock separated from the larger part of the company, which was taking the Fort Hall Road (Sublette's Cutoff). Goodbyes were said and the divided company members took last looks at each other as they followed their separated destinies. As others joined the party at different places on the Hastings Cutoff the company eventually grew to eighty-nine people.

The day after passing the Parting-of-the-Ways, the company held a meeting to elect leaders. The amiable "Uncle" George Donner, aged sixty-two, was elected to lead the company and the Donner Party was born. However, James Reed remained influential in the operations of the train. With the election over, the Donner Party pressed on toward Fort Bridger. There they expected to meet Hastings who had promised to guide the emigrants along his new wagon route.

Near the Little Sandy River, the Donner Party took in the unfortunate Luke Halloran. Halloran was already having a very bad journey. He was ill and had been abandoned by his previous traveling companions. Now here he was, taken in by what would become one of the unluckiest wagon companies in history. Fate was not smiling upon this unfortunate man. It is little surprise that poor Luke did not last much longer.

July 27, 1846 — Fort Bridger, Oregon Territory

The Donner Party proceeded across the windswept dune fields and sage flats of present-day Wyoming until, less than ten days later, they spotted the Bridger-Vasquez trading post, commonly called Fort Bridger. Here the group was able to trade worn livestock for fresh animals, buy goods, and visit the blacksmith for much-needed equipment repairs. Their anticipated meeting with Lansford Hastings did not happen. Hastings had left earlier with the Harlan-Young Party, headed for California over the Hastings Cutoff. The Donner wagon train had to move fast if they were to catch up with Hastings and his train.

At Fort Bridger, the Donner Party still had the option of taking the Oregon Trail to Fort Hall with little loss in time and far less risk. While at Fort Bridger, Jim Bridger, the famed mountain man, reinforced the notion that the Hastings Cutoff was the best route to California. It was in Bridger's financial interest to promote the Hastings Cutoff. Sublette's Cutoff had diverted traffic on the Oregon Trail so that it bypassed Fort Bridger, and the opening of Hastings' new route promised to return prosperity to the Bridger-Vasquez trading operations. Bridger filled the emigrants' ears with tales of how the Hastings Cutoff would indeed save them many miles. The story was a lie and Bridger most likely knew it. He had traveled widely in this portion of the West and was familiar with it like few others.

Church Buttes, near modern-day Granger, Wyoming was one of the many landmarks passed by the Donner Party.

> "Beyond Fort Britcher there are two roads, the old one past the so called Soda Springs and Fort Hall, and a new one called Captain Hastings' Cutoff which is said to be much shorter and passes by the Great Salt Lake. Many companies ahead of us had already chosen Hastings' Cutoff as their route, and we, too thought it preferable."
> (Heinrich Lienhard writing in the 1860s apparently editing a diary kept in 1846)

Bridger's tall tales carried the day and he convinced the Donner Party that it had made the right decision. They were about to discard their last option for an uneventful journey. Unbeknownst to the Donner Party, Bridger's partner, Louis Vasquez, held a letter to James F. Reed from Edwin Bryant. Mr. Bryant was an acquaintance of Reed who had gone over the Hastings Cutoff by mule train (the Russell-Bryant pack train) some time earlier. Prior to leaving Fort Bridger, he gleaned information from an individual familiar with the area and found out how rough the trail was likely to be. Bryant's own trip soon confirmed what he had heard. The letter warned Reed to stay off the Hastings Cutoff. Vasquez inexplicably never delivered this letter to Reed. Combined with his partner's evident duplicity in misrepresenting the terrain ahead, the failure to deliver the letter suggests Vasquez may have been in on the deception.

Despite Hastings' absence, the Donner Party had confidence in the man and the route. Reed wrote a letter to the *Sangamo Journal* from Fort Bridger. The letter indicated that the emigrants mistakenly believed themselves to be about "250 miles from California." Such distance normally required about three weeks of travel. Unfortunately completion of this "250 miles" took roughly eight months until the last of the party was rescued. The three weeks in which Reed expected to get to California would not see the party beyond even the Great Salt Desert; but at this moment, all was optimism. Reed wrote: "Mr. Bridger informs me that the route we design to take, is a fine level road with plenty of water and grass." The emigrants did not realize that Jim Bridger had reasons to lead them on.

The Donner Party stayed at Fort Bridger for four days, resting and refitting. The company was joined by the McCutchens from Missouri.[10] On July 31st the Donner Party headed west. An open letter from Hastings pointed the way for them to go. They felt confident they could follow Hastings and his company of sixty-six wagons. They followed the faint track left by Hastings's wagon train (the Harlan-Young Party) and others.[11] The trail was very rough. Ravines, ridges, and thick vegetation made the going difficult.

On August 6th the Donner Party found a tattered note left in a bush by Hastings. The note indicated that Hastings and his train were having trouble negotiating Weber Canyon and that they might not be able to make it through. Any who were following behind Hastings were encouraged to wait and send a messenger ahead. Hastings promised to come back and guide them through.

Three men, Pike, Reed, and Stanton, went on ahead to find Hastings. They found Hastings days later not far from the Great Salt Lake; but he refused to go back to guide the Donner Party through. Hastings went only as far as to take Reed to a summit in the Wasatch Mountains and attempt to point out a route that he believed would be better than the one the sixty- five wagons in the Harlan-Young Party had negotiated. On that route, one of the wagons had been wrecked. By recommending the Donner Party take a different and untried route Hastings was setting the Donner Party up for even more difficulties as the trusting emigrants were about to take a path previously untouched by wagon traffic.

> *"Our journey from Fort Bridger to Salt Lake was both difficult and disagreeable, especially when we had to travel through the sage-brush and greasewood. When we had come to within a half mile of the lake we halted at 'Weber canyon,' a pass which for about a mile and a half seemed impracticable. Our four head men held a council.*

---

10   The McCutchen family included William, Amanda, and Harriet.

11   The Harlan-Young Party was not the only group on the same track in 1846. The Hoppe Party (a.k.a. Lienhard Party) was shortly behind the Harlan-Young Party and was following their tracks. The name of this party is a matter of some contention as Lienhard and Hoppe actually had joined with a company under G.D. Dickenson. Taking the coward's way, out the coin toss came out in favor of calling this the Hoppe party in this book.

Reid and Donner turned, and trailed back for three days, and then crossed the mountains. We worked six days building a road, and got through on the seventh. This put Reid and Donner ten days behind us. If they had helped us we would have got through on the fourth day." (Jacob W. Harlan, member of the Harlan-Young Party writing in 1888)

Reed borrowed a horse and returned to the Donner camp with Hastings's advice. The delay had cost the Donner Party five precious days. This safety margin necessary to get through the Sierra Nevada Mountains was getting dangerously short. The Donner Party desperately needed the cooperation of Mother Nature to make it through before the snows arrived.[12]

August 11, 1846 — Wasatch Mountains, Above Great Salt Lake

The Donner Party left the trail cut by the Harlan—Young Party and set out on the route that Hastings had recommended even though he had never seen it. The trip took on new difficulties when the emigrants discovered that they had to cut the trail as they went. The thick underbrush, characteristic of the Wasatch Mountains, forced the road builders to cut and chop their way through the willow-choked canyons and sagebrush-covered flats. Additionally, portions of the route were steep and rocky, adding to the troubles of the twenty-seven men who were called upon to be road makers. Tempers began to flare.

The Donner Party was joined by the three wagons of the Graves/Fosdick family. These families brought John Snyder with them as a teamster. The additional relatively fresh workmen were welcome. The Donner Party now numbered eighty-seven souls.

Even with these reinforcements, the hacking of the trail up and down the mountains proceeded at a rate of only slightly more than a mile a day. Finally they crested the highest mountain and were able to glimpse the Great Salt Lake in the distance. But there

---

12 The youthful Harlan did not understand the predicament of the Donner Party. The Donner Party would have a much longer section of road to construct on their own. It creates an interesting "what-if" situation as to what would have happened had the Donners not followed Hastings' advice and followed the Harlan-Young party through Weber canyon. Both roads were rough but the Donners could have saved time by not having to cut their way through.

were more ridges and valleys to cross. The work slowed as the men fatigued. By August 20th the flagging emigrants had only made another six miles. On August 21st they abandoned the canyon route and pulled the wagons straight up a steep slope, which is now referred to as "Donner Hill" in Salt Lake City. This was a Herculean feat in itself.

In their struggles with the Wasatch Mountains, the Donner Party left a legacy. Much of their experiment in trailblazing would be used by the Mormons in their settlement of the Valley of the Great Salt Lake the following year. Mormon pioneers followed in their tracks as they sought to escape the prejudice of the dominant culture back east. Much of the route the Donner Party carved was expanded in 1847 and became a segment of the Mormon-Pioneer Trail.

Leaving a legacy, though, was the furthest thing from the minds of the California-bound emigrants. The cold in the night air warned of the coming winter. It was now becoming clear that the Donner Party was, if not in trouble, very close to it. They had covered only thirty-six miles in the fourteen days since they had waited for Reed to return with Hastings to guide them through. The emigrants should have covered somewhere between 140 and 180 miles in that time. Confidence in the word of Mr. Hastings began to plummet. Perhaps even Reed, an optimist just two weeks before, wondered about the decision to take Hasting's advice. The Donner Party had thrown away precious weeks and had worn down both the draft animals and the party members. The Donner Party could not easily push on in their current state; morale was flagging.

On August 25th the travelers camped near the Great Salt Lake, in the very campsite where Reed and Hastings had met before the struggle of the past two weeks. Perhaps Reed contemplated that the emigrants had, in a fortnight covered the same amount of distance he had traveled in less than three days by horseback. At least the pace had picked up that day, as the Donner Party traveled a greater distance than they had struggled through in the entire previous week.

Luke Halloran's frail health continued to deteriorate, and it was little surprise when later that evening, a wagon, trailing behind the others, rattled into camp with Luke's corpse in it. It is speculated that Luke died of consumption probably referring to tuberculosis or similar diseases. He was soon buried next to the grave of John Hargrave, a member of the Harlan-Young Party. A death, at the start of what all understood to be the most difficult part of the journey, was not auspicious. This also played on the minds of the emigrants. Among Luke's effects was discovered a fortune of roughly $1,500 in coin.

August 29, 1846 — Great Salt Desert, Mexico

In late August the Donner Party came to the most challenging section of the Hastings Cutoff-the Great Salt Desert. Although it must have been some consolation that this portion offered a fair walking route with no axe work to slow progress, it would be a long stretch without water, forage for the animals, or any protection from the elements. Deserts are often thought of as hot, but they are better characterized as extreme. The days often were scorching hot and the nights bitter cold. The wind stirred the sands into stinging clouds of sharp particles. Sections with loose and uncompacted sands engulfed wagon wheels and oxen hooves making forward progress almost impossible. Travel under such conditions was difficult even for well-rested and healthy people or animals. The Donner Party members and their animals already were in rough shape, and the Great Salt Desert might have easily put an end to the journey. Even in the early 21st century, this area is not to be taken lightly.

Fortune refused to smile on the Donner Party. One misfortune after another arose to test their mettle. One of Reed's wagons broke an axle, requiring a side trip of roughly fifteen miles to find replacement wood necessary for the repair. Even so, the going must have seemed almost easy compared with the ordeal of crossing the Wasatch Mountains. Water was a concern and many of the springs along the way were too salty to drink.

There are only so many times the travelers could reach down deep inside to draw upon those hidden reserves of strength. The Donner Party had stumbled into two such situations already on their journey and the worst was yet to come.

Several days after leaving the shores of the Great Salt Lake, the emigrants discovered a board with scraps of tattered paper attached:

"Close by the largest well stood a rueful spectacle-a bewildering guide board, flecked with bits of white paper, showing that the notice or message which had recently been pasted and tacked thereon had since been stripped off in irregular bits. In surprise and consternation, the emigrants gazed at its blank face, then toward the dreary waste beyond. Presently my mother knelt before it and began searching for fragments of paper, which she believed crows had wantonly pecked off and dropped to the ground.

Spurred by her zeal, others also were soon on their knees, scratching among the grasses and sifting the loose soil through their fingers. What they found, they brought to her and after the search ended she took the guide board, laid it across her lap, and thoughtfully began fitting the ragged edges of paper together and matching the scraps marks on the board. The tedious process was watched with spellbound interest by the anxious group around her. The writing was that of Hastings, and her patchwork brought out the following words: "2 days-2 nights-hard driving-cross desert - reach water." (Eliza Poor Donner Houghton writing in 1911)

Besides the message board, the travelers also found drinkable water available at this place. The emigrants decided to rest the oxen for a day and a half so that they could make the two-day push across the salt flats as rapidly as possible. After this rest, they moved out, following Hastings' faint wagon tracks. The trail took them over a series of ridges and salt flats. The going was extremely difficult. By the end of the second day of hard driving, they were still not quite halfway across the salt flats. The oxen and people tired rapidly and exhaustion was near. The thirsty travelers had all but exhausted their water barrels. Members of the party began to straggle as their stock played out. James Reed rode ahead to see if water could be found nearby. There was none.

They temporarily abandoned the wagons to drive the stock ahead to find water. Reed returned to his family and they managed to get one wagon out. They were no longer well-to-do but had to carry the few possessions they needed for survival. The remaining livestock packed food for the rest of the trip.

> "This desert had been represented to us as only forty miles wide but we found it nearer eighty. It was a dreary, desolate, alkali waste; not a living thing could be seen; it seemed as if the hand of death had been laid upon the country. We started in the evening, traveled all that night, and the following day and night-two nights and one day suffering from thirst and heat by day and piercing cold by night." (Virginia Reed Murphy writing in 1891)

On the fourth day of travel on the salt flats, the emigrants managed to get a few of their stock to water. After resting, these were driven back to the wagons, which were then moved west again. The loss of three-dozen oxen during the crossing of the salt flats was yet another disaster. With fewer animals to pull the load, the Donner Party had to abandon four wagons. Baggage, lovingly hauled more than thirteen hundred miles, was abandoned. Most of all, the desert caused the loss of more precious time; it was now early September. In more optimistic days, Reed had thought he would be starting his new life in California by this time. If there was not a change in luck soon, the emigrants might not get to California at all.

> "Our provisions were divided among the company. Before leaving the desert camp, an inventory of provisions on hand was taken, and it was found that the supply was not sufficient to last us through to California, and as if to render the situation more terrible, a storm came on during the night and the hilltops became white with snow." (Virginia Reed Murphy writing in 1891)

By the first week in September, snow on the hillsides foretold the likelihood that much of the remainder of the journey would combine freezing cold with treacherous travel conditions, but they had few options. It seemed they were past the point of no return and the only chance of survival they could see was to press on to California. The Donner Party members knew the Harlan-Young and Hoppe Parties were ahead of them. They counted on Hastings, the author of their predicament, to let the authorities in California know of their plight. The Harlan-Young and Hoppe Parties were sure to be far enough ahead to get through the mountains and send help if it was needed. The choice to press on put the Donner Party closer to both their destination and any help the Californians might offer. The Donner Party shouldered their burdens and the withered train of nineteen wagons continued west. They could still make out the faint track left by Hastings.

The wagons moved out early the next morning, driving relentlessly through the night and into the next day. Animals continued to drop from exhaustion and some had to be left behind. When the emigrants came to a well-watered meadow, they rested for an entire day. In recognition of the fact that it was likely the Donner Party could not traverse the mountains before winter set in, they decided to send men ahead to arrange for succor. They selected Charles Stanton and William McCutchen for this mission. These two set out on horseback while the remainder of the emigrants rested.

Though resting, the Donner Party was not idle. More property was disposed of and there was a shuffling of stock to balance the burdens. A leaner, better organized wagon company started out after their brief rest. Though sorely tested in the previous weeks, the leadership provided by James Reed and George Donner was sufficiently competent to retain group cohesion and keep the emigrants working together.

For a while, the terrain improved. Driving was easier. Water was available. The hunting was good. The Indians appeared to be friendly. The Hastings route took them many miles south to the Ruby Mountains (in present-day Nevada) and then north again to find a pass through the Diamond Mountains. On September 30th they finally crossed the Humboldt River. At last the Donner Party was off the damnable Hastings Cutoff and back on the main Oregon/California Trail. This "shortcut" had been somewhere between ten and ninety-five miles longer than the established trail routes! Even more costly than the extra distance was the substantial time lost in cutting a trail through the Wasatch Mountains. Instead of saving a month, it had added them a similar amount of time. It must have come as a great comfort to know that the remainder of their trek was along a tried and true wagon route.

The days were getting noticeably shorter and the chill of the night was deeper. Flocks of birds heading south appeared to announce winter's icy breath would be coming soon. There was more of an air of urgency to keep moving than ever. It was now October, and the Donner Party should already have arrived in California. They needed to push on to avoid being trapped in the mountains by early winter snow.

The Donner Party had several visits from Indians. One day a Native American helped to save several of the wagons from a brush fire. Here was a man who, the emigrants felt, had proved his trustworthiness. This individual joined the train and the emigrants gave him the name of "Thursday." Unlike Robinson Crusoe's man, "Friday," penned by Daniel Dafoe, this fellow had ulterior motives. He and another Native American were allowed to camp with the party. In the morning they were gone along with several pieces of property, including two precious oxen.

The Donner Party pushed on as fast as they could. They averaged roughly twenty miles a day now. For a wagon train, this was much akin to taking wings and flying. The fact that they could make this pace shows the conditioning, which the party had attained since the start of the journey. There were no weaklings left. The increase in the daily rate of travel was partially due to the lightening of the burden for the remaining oxen. The Donner Party had cast out much of its valuable property and the wagons carried little but the essentials. The rapidity of their journey also reflected the fact that the emigrants were now very serious about making as much forward progress in a day as possible. As it is doubtful the average speed of the oxen increased dramatically the remarkable increase likely was attained by increasing the hours of walking.

October 5, 1846 — Along the Humboldt River

The long days of walking were wearing thin on people already pushed to the limit, as evidenced by an incident that cost the life of John Snyder. On October 5th the emigrants struggled up yet another in the almost endless series of hills. The real cause of the flare in tempers is unclear. Two of the teams became tangled and John Snyder began to beat the oxen. There are varied accounts of what happened next.

One version suggests that when James Reed tried to talk Snyder into cooling off, Snyder threatened him with a whipping as well.[13] Reed drew a knife and Snyder responded by striking him with the whip. Within a split second Reed's knife was in Snyder's chest. Snyder continued to flail at Reed with the whip, but the knife wound was fatal.

William C. Graves, one of the few survivors to see the fight, describes a different version.

> *"Just then Reed had got another team to double to his wagon, and started to pass Snider's wagon; but the leaders did not want to pass, and tangled in Snider's oxen. Reed at this time was on the opposite side of the oxen from Snider, and said to Snider, "you have no business here in the way;" Snider said, "it is my place." Reed started toward him, and jumping over the wagon tongue, said, "you are a damned liar, and I'll cut your heart out!" Snider pulled his clothes open on his breast and said, "cut away." Reed ran to him and stuck a large six-inch butcher's knife into his heart and cut off two ribs. Snider then turned the butt-end of his whip stock and struck at him three times, but missed him the third and hit Mrs. Reed, who had in the meantime got hold of her husband." (William C. Graves writing in 1877)*

The emigrants camped and considered their next course of action. Had the entire group not had such frayed nerves, it is possible that they would have waited to turn Reed over to the authorities in California. There was much talk about what to do. Louis Keseberg wanted to hang Reed there and then from his

---

13   There are multiple versions of the killing of Snyder. According to J.W. Harlan, Reed told a tale where the knifing occurred after a heated exchange wherein Snyder clubbed Reed several times with a whip handle. All that is clear is that Reed stabbed Snyder. The murder reflected as much about the overall state of morale in the party as it did about the antagonists. This moment of anger had profound effects upon the futures of all the emigrants.

wagon tree (tongue). Finally it was agreed that Reed must leave the train. He was banished! The next morning Reed left on an almost skeletal horse with no weapons. Some, no doubt, thought that this would carry out the desired death sentence. However, Reed's family managed to get weapons to him, and he was made of sterner stuff than the others suspected. His survival turned out to be one of their better bits of luck.

> "I had determined to stay with him, and begged him to let me stay, but he would listen to no argument, saying it was impossible. Finally unclasping my arms from around him, he placed me in charge of Elliot, who started back to camp with me - and papa was left alone." (Virginia Reed Murphy writing in 1891)

Things were not easy for Reed. He left the main party alone with a worn-out horse. Shortly later, though, Walter Herron, a teamster for the Reed family, joined him in his exile. The two pressed on to California as rapidly as possible. Despite having but one horse, they made good time. The travelers far outstripped the plodding wagon train, but their supplies ran out well short of their destination and Reed kept the two alive by hunting wild game with the guns smuggled to him by his family. The two were in such dire straits that, when pressing through the Sierras, they scoured the trail for individual beans and scraps of food dropped by previous travelers.

> "We soon reached ransacked and abandoned wagons, hoping to find something to eat, but found nothing. Taking the tar bucket that was hanging under one of the wagons, I scraped the tar off and found a streak of rancid tallow at the bottom. I remember well that when I announced what I had found, Herren, who was sitting on a rack near by, got up, following with all the strength he had, and came to me. I handed the tar paddle to him, having some of the tallow about the size of a walnut on it. This he swallowed without giving it a smell. I then took a piece myself, but it was very repulsive .... After leaving the wagons probably fifty yards, I became deadly sick and blind." (James Reed writing in 1871)

Reed recovered and shortly after the incident and the toxic tallow apparently left Herron unaffected. The two discovered emigrants and wagons in the Bear Valley. They had made it! Soon they would be safe at Sutter's Fort, near modern Sacramento. There, the two men would be in a position to send help back to the others before it was too late.

Back on the trail, trouble with Indians continued to plague the wagon train's westward movement. The emigrants were alarmed when they found a note left by the exiled Reed, which warned that earlier emigrants had a battle with Indians nearby.

> "We found a board sticking by the side of the trail warning emigrants that the Indians were hostile and dangerous. It stated that on the previous day Governor Boggs' party had a severe fight with the Indians; that one man named Salley was killed in the fight, and Ben Lippincott badly wounded; they had killed about forty Indians; that the savages fought with poisoned arrows, tipped with the venom of a rattlesnake; that many Indians had concentrated at this point to steal stock, and murder emigrants, and that they had buried Salley in the road, and run the wagons over the grave to conceal it. Notwithstanding these precautions, a few rods past this notice we found poor Salley's body. The savages found the grave, dug him up, scalped him, and mutilated his body in a cruel manner." (Jacob W. Harlan member of the Harlan-Young Party writing in 1888) [14]

An even more ominous sign that they were in the vicinity of hostile Indians was the discovery along the trail of the skeletal remains of a member of an earlier party, who had apparently died of an arrow wound. This was a sobering sign. The threat of attack by Indians temporarily mended many of the tears in the fabric of the society of the travelers. Without Reed to hold the company together, the wagon company dispersed, often camping miles apart. The perception of dangers from Indians reunited the wagon train.

---

14 Harlan's recollection contains fanciful items such as the number of Indians shot and the venom-tipped arrowheads. The exhumation and mutilation of emigrant corpses is an often-documented occurrence. Cloth was a valuable commodity, even the cloth from a dead body.

Their troubles continued to mount, the reunited company still made an easy target for Indians, who ran off with some of the remaining horses. The emigrants left another wagon behind. Food was in short supply. Forage for the animals was poor. Yet the walking skeletons continued their march. The Donner Party had yet to reach the Humboldt Sink. As the emigrants proceeded, Indians harassed them and wounded many of the stock.

Although the Donner Party had suffered and worked together through a host of hardships, it rapidly became a situation in which each family looked out only for itself. The Donner Party was an organized wagon company in name only. Instead of working together to overcome difficulties, as had been the case when Reed effectively served as their captain, each new struggle and misfortune amplified the normal tensions of moving and camping together.

The erosion of social ties continued, and there seemed to be little sympathy for one another. As an example of the mood of the travelers, even as the wagon company found itself being hounded by Indians, Louis Keseberg cast the aged Mr. Hardcoop out to fend for himself. Someone else sent a rider back for the old man, but shortly after Hardcoop returned to the company, Keseberg again turned him out. This time the old man was left to die of exposure along the trail. None of the others went back to save him from certain death. He was never heard from again.

October 12, 1846 — *Humboldt Sink, Province of Mexico*

On October 12th and through the early hours of the thirteenth, the emigrants drove hard to the Humboldt Sink. They reached the sink in the dead of night, having lost an animal or two in the latest exhausting drive. As they settled down to rest, Indians attacked the train and shot twenty-one head of livestock. Some oxen were dead, many were badly wounded. There was little to do but butcher the dead and slaughter the severely wounded animals. The meat began to spoil rapidly as there was no way to preserve it aside from the long process of drying. There was no time to dry all the meat. The emigrants had to move on before the snows came in earnest.

The party could now move only fifteen wagons. They ate what they could of the supplies that would be otherwise abandoned and moved on. Wolfinger, Reinhard, and Spitzer remained behind to cache goods. They planned to follow later. Indians laughed from their hiding places as the much-reduced procession of emigrants moved by. What more could possibly go wrong?

The emigrants pressed on through the hellish desert. The loss of livestock continued. More possessions were cached or thrown away. Tempers continued to flare as water and food grew scarce. Finally they came to the Truckee River. They had crossed the final desert! The cost had been high in livestock, lives, individual strength, and morale. Still, a great expanse of mountains loomed ominously ahead.

With the desert behind them, the weary Donner Party rested for a day. They had been averaging roughly twenty miles a day in their last push and they needed to gather strength for the next difficult mountain stretch. After this brief respite, they moved forward and were shortly into rough terrain with many river crossings. Spitzer and Reinhard, who had remained behind to cache goods, caught up with the party at this point. According to their tale, Indians killed Wolfinger and burned the wagons.[15] There was nothing to do but mourn another lost companion and move on.

A number of expeditions were attempted to help the stranded emigrants. The first two were relief expeditions that simply tried to bring supplies and assistance; later efforts were rescue expeditions that were intended to take the stranded emigrants on across the mountains to California.

First Relief Expedition[16]

On October 19th the party met Charles Stanton, one of the

---

15   As will be seen later, the Indians were falsely accused. Wolfinger died as a result of treachery from within his own emigrant company.

16   To make better sense out of the numerous assistance expeditions mounted the following convention is applied. A relief expedition is meant to bring supplies to sustain the emigrants as they continue their journey. A rescue expedition is meant to bring out people, recognizing that the emigrants are unable to proceed without physical assistance. A salvage expedition is meant to bring out property. Previous works have mixed all these intended purposes under the rubric of relief. The first party was a relief expedition, even though the emigrants were not yet trapped.

men the emigrants had sent ahead for help. Stanton had with him seven mules loaded with provisions from Sutter's Fort. Accompanying Stanton were two of Sutter's Indian vaqueros, Luis and Salvador. The emigrants were jubilant at this good fortune.

Though William McCutchen had taken ill and stayed behind in California, he had helped procure these most-welcome provisions from John Sutter. The relief party also brought news that James Reed and Walter Herron had made it through to California. They brought welcomed fresh supplies but most of all they brought hope.

> "...here we met Stanton, one of the men we had sent after provisions, he had two California Indians with him and five mules packed with flour and jerked beef; he told us to go slow and recruit our teams, so they could pull us over the mountains, for they were very rough; that there would be no danger of snow, for others could cross in midwinter and we could do the same, so we did as he said, and lost five days between here and the mountains..." (William C. Graves writing in 1877)[17]

The emigrants rested easily, consuming the food from Sutter and preparing for the end of the journey. The vaqueros suggested that heavy snows were not expected for some time, so it seemed reasonable to recruit their strength before tackling the mountain passes. Just when all seemed to be going right, William Pike was struck by an accidental pistol discharge and died.[18]

As the party laid Pike in his grave, a gentle snow began to fall. The travelers had tarried there five days, in hindsight several days too long. It was time to move on. Those with more-rested stock moved on ahead. The Donner Party, as a cohesive group, had dissolved. It was becoming a situation of every family for itself.

---

17   Graves does not recall the correct number of mules but does manage to ascribe some blame to their helpers for the fatal delay that would keep them trapped on the wrong side of the mountain pass.

18   There are conflicting accounts as to whether Pike was killed while cleaning his own pistol or by an accidental discharge of Foster's pistol which was in the process of being loaded. Given the almost complete lack of safety features on pistols of the period such accidents were common amongst emigrants.

The Reeds on the eastern side of the mountains no longer had to worry that the next bend in the trail might lead them to the corpse of the family patriarch. Additionally the family knew that James Reed would never let them down. He would make sure California was aware of their distress.

Stanton provided accurate information as to what the road ahead was like; for the first time since departing Fort Bridger, the travelers knew what terrain to expect. At the first night's rest, an Indian began showering the cattle with arrows. The assailant hit nineteen oxen before William Eddy shot him with his rifle. None of the livestock were killed, but the wounds were serious enough for animals already approaching their physical limits.

Pleasant Valley, Truckee River.

The Truckee River represented the end of the deserts the Donner Party had to cross. The toll taken to get this far did not leave the Donner Party with sufficient strength to easily cross the mountains looming high above the river before the snows shut them in.

Hell Freezes Over

Winter's Coming On

"Winter had set in a month earlier than usual. All trails and roads were covered; and our only guide was the summit which it seemed we would never reach. Despair drove many nearly frantic. That night came the dreaded snow. Around the camp-fires under the trees great feathery flakes came whirling down. The air was so full of them that one could see objects only a few feet away." (Virginia Reed Murphy writing in 1891)

The temperatures continued to drop and snow dusted them each day. The mountains ahead donned a cloak of white. The emigrants knew they needed to hurry on, but it seemed something always happened to slow them to a crawl. A Donner wagon broke an axle and George Donner suffered a debilitating gash attempting to repair the wagon. The emigrants once again separated as Breen pioneered the route for those who wished to press on while George Donner rested. The Donners and their entourage followed behind later as the others struggled to get through the mountains. On All Hallows' Eve (October 31st), at the head of the procession the Breen family halted for the night within a short pull of being through the crest of the mountain pass. The ground had snow on it and the clouds looked heavy.

They spent a miserable night on the snow hoping to make a way through in the morning. With the rising of the sun it was clear that the night's weather had made that wish all but impossible. Roughly a foot of fresh snow had fallen. The winds whipped the snow into drifts ten or more feet deep. There was nothing to do now but return the way they came. The emigrants slowly dusted the snow off and plodded back down the trail. What to do? What to do?

There was little choice now but to make a winter camp and hope for a rescue or a major thaw. After all, the word of their plight was already known in California. Certainly Reed, Herron, and McCutchen, safe in California, knew the party was trapped and in peril of perishing without assistance. The emigrants prayed the Californians would not let them down and would arrange for help to reach them.

The disappointed Breen family returned to the eastern end of Truckee Lake. There they found Moses Schallenberger's abandoned cabin[19] and a supply of timber. They used the latter to build two more cabins. Nearly sixty people gathered in these cabins waiting optimistically for the early snows to melt.

The Truckee Lake Camp,[20] hereafter called the "Lake Camp," which housed most of the emigrants and was led by the Breens, offered an abundant supply of water and wood, both of which had been scarce for long periods of the journey. There was the shell of one cabin already completed. When it was clear that they could not get through until the snows melted, the emigrants set about preparing for winter with a purpose. Many believed the snow would soon melt, and that perhaps explains why the cabins were not more substantial. The cabins were very rough and relied upon canvas and skins to keep the roofs weatherproof. While two new cabins were constructed, the existing Schallenberger cabin was made more serviceable.

George Donner and his family had not yet made it to Truckee Lake when the heavy snows forced him to set up a tent camp at Alder Creek, hereafter referred to as the "Alder Creek Camp." This encampment site was roughly five miles from the Breens cabin.

---

19 In 1844 deep snows trapped a wagon company on the eastern flank of the mountain, much like the Donner Party in 1846. Moses Schallenberger and two companions (Joseph Foster and Allen Montgomery) had volunteered to stay behind and guard wagons which could not get through the pass. They built a cabin on the Truckee Lake, that played a large role in the Donner Party saga. As food supplies dwindled, in December of 1844 the three tried to walk to safety using snowshoes. Moses could not make it and went back to the cabin to wait out the winter. In February of 1845 he was rescued by another snowshoer.

20 The Lake Camp encompassed three separate locales spread over one-half mile. The cabins were not near each other as one might expect. The divisions between the members of the company continued to push them apart. It is best to consider the camp as a cluster of separate wintering areas rather than a coherent community.

The Donner group never completed a real cabin but constructed three crude huts to house twenty-one people.

Shelter was only one of the problems the emigrants needed to solve. The food problem was the most difficult. The hard feelings between group members combined with the lack of effective leadership meant that there was no communal plan for sharing such resources as they had. One family might have an excess of a commodity, such as salt, and another might be in need of it. In the final analysis, however, no one was sitting on a treasure trove of food. In the end, time would assure that all were reduced to extreme want.

The trapped emigrants tried hunting and fishing with no luck, except for a less-than-wily coyote, a few ducks, a bear, a squirrel, and an owl. Killing the bear almost cost William Eddy his life, but the bear provided several hundred pounds of meat and a useful hide.

The hunters from both camps helped the overall situation but could not provide enough to feed more than eighty people for long. The emigrants were quickly down to starvation rations. They slaughtered oxen and stored the meat. Since the cold was constant now, they used nature's deep freeze to preserve the meat. The slaughtering of the draft animals was the surest sign that the emigrants' hope for a thaw to open the pass was gone.

As the days wore on, the other animals, including the family dogs, found themselves killed and thrown into the cooking pot. The supplies were running out fast. The only things in great supply were snow, water, wood, and despair.

The Second Relief Expedition

While the emigrants were settling into their winter camps, down in California, Reed, who had been banished for the killing of John Snyder, and McCutchen made plans for a second relief expedition. However, the effects of the War with Mexico and the Bear Flag Rebellion made it difficult to find sufficient men, equipment, and supplies to mount an effective mission. Most of the able-bodied men were serving in the militia or otherwise engaged in the war. Surprisingly James Reed volunteered to fight and raise soldiers for the war. He was elected captain of his military company but would only accept the post of lieutenant. This is a clear example of how little he understood what his family was up against.

Reed had passed Stanton's First Relief Expedition on his way to Sutter's Fort so he had little doubt that the foodstuffs provided by Sutter had been delivered, but he knew the supplies would be exhausted within a few days. Regardless of how Reed may have felt about the remainder of the emigrants in the Donner Party, he was sorely worried about his wife and children. He expected that the emigrants were over the divide by now but in poor straits. Reed did not know that soon the party would hold up in two separate camps on the opposite side of the mountains. If he and William McCutchen knew the actual situation faced by the Donner Party, no doubt, they would have organized with more haste.

Reed and McCutchen, accompanied by two Indian vaqueros, started on a simple mission to bring foodstuffs to their hungry families but this metamorphosed into a desperate errand to stave off potential starvation. They packed supplies onto twenty-six horses. On October 30th this tiny relief mission set out. The men slogged ahead to Johnson's Ranch, north of Sutter's Fort and close to the mountain trail. At the ranch they acquired four more horses and a mule, rested for three days, and then headed up the trail.

As the relief party moved east, the weather worsened. Rain turned into sleet and sleet into snow. When they reached the Bear Valley, where Reed expected to find the party, the wagons were not there! The sickening realization that the emigrants were on the other side of the Sierras hit the relief party. The relief party moved slowly now, hindered by two feet of snow. They met two emigrants from another train, Mr. and Mrs. Jotham Curtis, who were snowbound in a crude shelter. The Curtises were on the verge of starvation, being reduced to consuming their family dog for dinner. Reed and his party feasted on the unfortunate canine and shared some of the relief supplies with the emigrants. The next morning Reed and McCutchen left nine horses and one of the vaqueros with the Curtises. The plan was that the Curtises would be taken to safety when the relief party returned with the Donner Party.

The relief party continued their nearly impossible trek. The slope was steep and covered with three feet of powder snow. They managed only three miles the first day. That night their remaining Indian companion deserted. McCutchen retraced his steps to the Curtis camp to find the vaquero had deserted and taken three horses. With iron endurance, McCutchen returned to rejoin Reed.

The next morning the two pushed on. Snow was falling and now exceeded four feet in many places. Their pack animals began to give out; and when the last one collapsed, they pressed on with only their saddle horses. These animals shortly gave out as well. With all the beasts of burden gone, they forged through shoulder-deep snow on foot. Eventually they realized that if they continued in their current condition the Donner Party would more likely be relieving them than vice versa. They could bring no succor, only two more mouths to feed. It was time to turn back.

Reed and McCutchen dug the surviving animals out of the snowdrifts and headed back to the Curtis camp. Here they cached many of the supplies, hoping to use this area as a depot for another relief mission or perhaps even a rescue expedition. The relief party took the Curtises to safety. Although a failure in their primary goal, the party accomplished some good. Reed, upon his return to Sutter's Fort, tried to arrange for another expedition. There simply were no men to be had and there was little chance of traversing the snows until sometime in February. The Donner Party had no option but to get by on their own resources until then! Back in the mountains the snows continued to pile up.

Escape Attempts

While the emigrants waited for help from California, they sought every opportunity to help themselves escape their winter camps. On November 12th, after a brief thaw, a few of the Lake Camp occupants attempted to break through the snow blockade. The conditions of travel were so exhausting and the snows so deep that they returned to the camp in a few hours. They were convinced that there would be other chances to escape. It was just a matter of time before they could get through.

It was not until November 21st that there was another break in the weather. For more than a week, the snows had been thawing, and twenty-two of the Lake Camp emigrants, employing seven mules, made an attempt to get through the pass. After a day they had made it across! The snows remained deep on the other side, but the emigrants had gone so far already. Nevertheless, exhaustion and the lack of food played heavily upon them. The mules made poor progress. Stanton, Luis, and Salvador refused to go forward and it was imperative that one of them guide the others. The snow began to fall again. The crestfallen party returned to their cabins late that night. Planning began for the next attempt almost immediately.

November 25th brought more rain and snow. The ground around the cabins was melted free of snow for a brief period. But always another snow squall came and blanketed the landscape. By November 30th Patrick Breen recorded in his diary that there were between four and five feet of snow on the ground.

During this period, several of the oxen, horses, and mules, that had not yet been slaughtered, wandered away and died of exposure. This was a major disaster, as the snow-covered carcasses were invisible in the gleaming landscape of snowdrifts, which surrounded the winter camps. The snow was by this time more than eight feet deep and the last reserve between the Donner Party and starvation had been cruelly taken from them and buried under their very noses. That meat would be missed in the coming months. It was only the end of November, still several weeks before the start of winter. Where were the rescuers? Perhaps hell is not an eternal fire but an eternity of gnawing cold and hunger.

Though the snows continued to pile up, the emigrants still entertained thoughts of making their own way through the mountains to safety. Some of them had seen snowshoes and resolved to manufacture this footgear for the next escape attempt. Fourteen pairs of snowshoes were produced. While this was going on, the weather and lack of nutrition wreaked havoc on the emigrants' health. Shortly before departure time for the desperate escape attempt, the slow death which haunted their nightmares arrived as Bayliss Williams died. It was clear that poor Bayliss was but leading the way for more to follow.

The Forlorn Hope

> "Finally a party was organized, since known as "Forlorn Hope." ... They were over a month on the way, and the horrors endured by that Forlorn Hope no pen can describe nor imagination conceive." (Virginia Reed Murphy writing in 1891)

The new escape plan called for Stanton, Luis, and Salvador to guide the snowshoers through. The party included almost every able-bodied person remaining, including ten men, five women, and two boys.[21] The party was mostly drawn from the Lake Camp but included individuals from both camps.[22] A few fit individuals remained in the camps on the lake and Alder Creek. There remaining fit emigrants tended children, ill, and injured.

This party, often called the "Forlorn Hope," waited until the waning days of fall for a break in the storms. Fair weather finally came, and on December 16th the party moved out. Since only fourteen people had snowshoes, those without traveled at the tail end of the procession in the paths made by the others. Progress for the starving party was slow. Two members, Charles Burger and William Murphy, turned back before completing the four miles covered the first day. When night came, the freezing emigrants had no recourse but to settle down for an uncomfortable night of camping in the snow. This was no small feat. Campfires built on the snow quickly extinguished themselves as the fire melted the snow underneath. The snowshoers experimented to come up with a solution to this problem. Once the emigrants figured out that they could erect a substantial crib or platform on the snow to build the fire upon, they huddled around the life-preserving flames for the night. They had no tents or shelter.

---

21 The band was comprised of Antonio, Charles Burger, Patrick Dolan, William Eddy, Jay Fosdick, Sarah Fosdick, Sarah Foster, William Foster, Franklin Graves, Mary Graves, Amanda McCutchen, Luis, Lemuel Murphy, William Murphy, Harriet Pike, Salvador, and Charles Stanton.

22 Charles Burger had moved from Alder Creek to the Lake Camp. Antonio may have been residing at Alder Creek when the expedition left.

The second day they made it through the pass. The third day was downhill, but progress remained difficult. Some of the party were afflicted with snow blindness. As they walked, brief snow squalls stung their faces. They struggled for roughly six miles that third day.

The fourth day brought the first signs of hypothermia. There were now hallucinations to deal with. The party slowed to five miles for a day's walking. The food in their packs dwindled to one more day's supply. The next day brought the official start of winter.

On the sixth morning Stanton was played out. He said he would follow but stayed behind as the party staggered onward. He did not rejoin the group after being abandoned. Had they but known about it, the party was within easy distance of the food left by Reed and McCutchen in their abortive relief attempt earlier that fall. Blindly they stumbled forward, but the snows made it difficult to read the trail; and they took the wrong path.

Each day the situation worsened. On the seventh day (December 23rd) the food was all but gone. The next day, a heavy storm hit the unfortunates. Despair grew and the hallucinations continued. They could hardly go onward. The Forlorn Hope had been without food for two days. In these dire straits, the topic of conversation turned to cannibalism. There were discussions of killing one of their number for food. There was a proposal about letting members have a shoot out and eating the loser. Eddy apparently convinced the group that nature would soon enough provide a corpse. They waited as their stomachs growled with hunger.

The eighth day was Christmas Eve. That night the emigrants were not as careful as they had been on previous nights in building a wooden platform to support their fire. The fire sank several feet into the snow pack, until it was extinguished when one of the Indians apparently bumped into its precarious perch and knocked it into the pool of icy water. Eddy probably saved most of those present by forcing them to move out of the pit melted by the fire and spoon together in the snow bank above in an improvised tent. [23]   Antonio apparently died early in the evening. The snow covered them over that night and Franklin Ward (Uncle Billy) Graves died by morning.

The storm continued through Christmas Day. Patrick Dolan died toward evening. The emigrants continued to stay in their shelter without food, water, or fire for the day. On the 26th Eddy bestirred his strength to start a fire. Unfortunately he used gunpowder to get the fire started. In the process his powder horn exploded, burning him severely. A second attempt to start a fire finally succeeded.

Finally, the will to survive won out over cultural taboo for all save Eddy, Luis, and Salvador. Patrick Dolan's corpse was butchered and roasted on the fire. The two Native Americans reconsidered this strategy and ate human flesh on the following day. Eddy continued to live off scraps of bear meat he had kept hidden. The emigrants tried to regain strength for their escape.

> *"Father died on Christmas night at eleven o'clock in the commencement of the snow storm. During that storm we had neither fire nor food. When it was over (leaving four of our number there,) and travelled on until the 5th of January, subsisting on human flesh." (Mary Graves writing in 1847)*

The survivors in the snowshoe party grew stronger on the remains of their dead comrades. On December 30th they moved on, even though they were hopelessly lost. William Eddy finally succumbed to the need for food and that evening consumed human flesh for the first time.

On New Year's Eve the snowshoers finally saw past the snowfields to the distant green valleys beyond. On New Year's Day the food ran out again. Jay Fosdick was failing fast and the group did not know whether to leave him behind or drag him

---

23   Spooning is a custom whereby individuals keep warm by sleeping while nestled against another person or persons. Sometimes a group of people might nestle together on the ground appearing like a stack of spoons against each other, hence the derivation for the term. For those camping shelterless in the snow with but few blankets, it would have been imperative to keep from freezing to death. Unlike today, sleeping with other people did not necessarily imply sexual meanings and it was recognized as a perfectly respectable manner in which to spend a cold night.

along. They were now eating rawhide from their shoes, but they kept Fosdick with them.

On January 4th, with hallucinations continuing in their hypothermic minds, the emigrants discussed killing and eating their two Native American companions, Salvador and Luis. The two Native Americans, overhearing or suspecting the fate being prepared for them, disappeared from camp.

Later that day William Eddy and Mary Graves followed the general direction of the trail made by Luis and Salvador. Ostensibly they were hunting other game as the country was now more open. William and Mary stumbled upon a deer and killed it. Quickly they built a fire and gorged themselves upon the animal. Eddy tried to signal the others with his rifle. He was unable to bring fresh meat to the other snowshoers before Jay Fosdick died. Though they had fresh venison provided by Eddy, the emigrants removed Fosdick's organs for future consumption. This they accomplished over the strenuous objections of Mrs. Fosdick. The emigrants spent the day resting, eating both the deer and Fosdick.

The next day the Forlorn Hope Party continued on, the going getting rougher with each step. That night William Foster suggested that he and Eddy kill Mrs. McCutchen for food as he thought she was an unpleasant person. Eddy was horrified and as Foster continued to weigh the merits of killing one member of the party over another, he and Eddy got into a fight. Foster was only saved from Eddy's knife by the ladies, one of whom Foster had been considering murdering. Social cohesion was at its nadir.

They now were edging out of the snow packs. As the emigrants continued their journey, they saw fresh footprints of two men. William Foster, knowing it was Luis and Salvador, set out on the trail to kill them. He found the two Native Americans nearly played out. Though Eddy spoke up to save their lives, no one raised a hand to save poor Luis and Salvador. There was no repeat of the fight between Eddy and Foster that had occurred when the latter wished to kill the women. Foster coldly shot both helpless men. These men had come to bring help to a party of strangers and were rewarded with murder. Foster was now completely out of control and the remaining travelers, including his own family member, would not camp with him.

> "Two Indians were killed, whose flesh lasted until we got out of the snow and came where Indians lived. Thence we subsisted nine days on acorns." (Mary Graves writing in 1847)

The trip continued and the emigrants subsisted on grasses and little else. Finally, on January 12th, they spied an Indian village. The villagers gave the starving travelers acorn bread and directions to safety. The emigrants, who had shown no mercy to the two starving Native Americans in their party, were civilly received by several Indian villages over the next several days. On January 17th the five women and Foster gave out. They refused to go farther. William Eddy, ever the indomitable, pressed on until he arrived at the settlement called Johnson's Ranch. He was rescued!

Eddy told the people at Johnson's Ranch the location of the survivors of the Forlorn Hope Party and food was taken to the women and Foster. They all were to be brought to safety the next morning! The news was spread far and wide. There were survivors from the Donner Party. Of the fifteen people who had not turned back, seven had made it through. All of the women had survived, a matter that leads to much speculation concerning the survivability and toughness of one gender over the other. However it is clear that without Eddy's heroic efforts there likely would not have been a single survivor of the Forlorn Hope.

Christmas in the Camps

Those who had not gone with the Forlorn Hope Party were still in the camps on the east side of the pass. We are fortunate that Patrick Breen's diary of events in the winter camps survived to provide an eyewitness chronicle of events. Breen tells us that the snow piled up rapidly, reaching a depth of roughly nine feet by December 19th. This severely restricted the mobility of the emigrants, making most of these days an ordeal of being confined and hungry. It appears that many of them spent most of the day in bed. Furthermore, the deepening snowdrifts made it less likely that any of the missing livestock could be found and used for food.

Christmas came and went with little fanfare. In the camps, the holiday meals consisted of beans and tripe as well as oxtail soup. There was much praying and Margaret Reed did what she could to prepare a proper feast for the children. As another storm hit, perhaps the emigrants considered the fate of those in the snowshoe party, who had been gone since December 16th.

As the dwindling food crisis deepened, the emigrants cooked the last of the dogs. Families relied upon boiled hides for much of their subsistence. Anything that could be scavenged from the old trash heaps was a blessing. Procuring wood became a problem and visits between the scattered camps became less frequent.

> "We had to kill littel cash the dog & eat him we ate his entrails and feet & hide & evry thing about him o my Dear Cousin you dont now what trubel is yet. Many a time we had the last thing a cooking and did not know wher the next would come from but there was awl weis some way provided there was 15 in the cab on we was in and half of us had to lay a bed all the time thare was 10 starved to death then we was hadly abel to walk we lived on little cash a week and after Mr. Breen would cook his meat we would take the bones and boil them 3 or 4 days at a time." (Letter of Virginia Reed to her cousin shortly after her rescue, May 16, 1847)

Before the new year arrived, Jacob Donner, Joseph Reinhard, Sam Shoemaker, James Smith, and Charles Burger died. The men were fading away very fast. Before he died, Reinhard admitted to the crime of killing Mr. Wolfinger back at Humboldt Sink. There was little good news to usher in the new year. However, there was hope that the passing of 1846 would see an end to the continuing problems that had besieged the emigrants.

> "Thursday 31st Last of the year, may we with Gods help spend the coming year better than the past which we propose to do if Almighty God will deliver us from our present dreadful situation which is our prayer if the will of God sees it fiting for us Amen." (Patrick Breen diary entry of December 31, 1846)

Margaret Reed, Virginia Reed, Eliza Williams, and Milt Elliot were determined to try their hands at making a breakout. On January 4th, this pitiful escape party set out. Eliza gave out after one night and turned back. The remainder of the party lasted two more nights, lost in the frozen wilderness. By January 8th, all were back in their cabins. How fortunate they all were, because two nights later another huge winter storm bore down on the emigrants. By January 13th, the snows in the Lake Camp were more than thirteen feet deep. No doubt the four emigrants would have perished had they been away from the cabins when the storm hit. Virginia Reed had frostbitten feet, but all were in relatively good health considering the ordeal they had endured.

The huge storm made life even more miserable. The emigrants were all but confined to their stuffy quarters. There was much praying, some storytelling, Bible reading, and conversation to while away the frozen hours. Young Louis Keseberg died. Mrs. Murphy lost her vision. Others of the party were fading fast. By the end of the month John Landrum Murphy died. Would help never come?

Aquilla Glover and the First Rescue Party

As soon as they were brought to safety, the survivors of the Forlorn Hope considered what to do next. Eddy sent a letter ahead to Alcade John Sinclair, asking for help for those remaining in the mountains. Mrs. Sinclair responded by sending clothes back to the rescued women and referring the matter to the commander of the local fort, Lieutenant Edward M. Kern.[24] Originally three men Sept Mootry, Aquilla Glover, and Joe Foster[25] agreed to go for the exorbitant wages of three dollars a day. Upon his return, Sinclair put his personal fortune behind the expedition and, with help from John Sutter, raised four more men.

At the end of January, a party of seven rescuers moved out of Sutter's Fort. Aquilla Glover was in charge of this group and they used a break in the weather to press on as rapidly as possible. The would-be rescuers picked up additional

---

24 Also referred to as "Captain Kerns."

25 Sept Mootry was also known as Riley Septimus Moultry and Joe Foster was also known as Joseph Sels. The later additions to this group were Edward Coffeemeyer (also spelled Coffeymire and Coffemeir), Daniel Rhodes, John Rhodes, and Reasin P. Tucker (also spelled Reason).

members at Johnson's Ranch and numbered fourteen[26] when they set out from there on February 4th. Glover's men were an interesting bunch and included in their number Donner Party member William Eddy, who had been at Sutter's Fort barely two weeks since leading the Forlorn Hope out of the mountains.

Traveling through rain, the rescuers made barely ten miles the first day. As they reached the mountains, the weather worsened. On February 5th, the rain fell in torrents. So much rain came that the party was forced to stop and build a platform to keep the supplies off the wet ground. Water stood two to three inches deep and still it continued to pour for another day and night. It was not until the February 8th that they could move on.

The rain left a legacy of swollen streams and mud. At one stream crossing, a small meandering brook turned into a one hundred-foot-wide river. It took half the day to carefully get the men and the precious pack animals across. Within a few miles of this crossing, the men found themselves in a field of snow three or more feet deep. The great storms had depressed the snow line considerably and the chances of reaching the stranded emigrants were growing slimmer with each passing moment.

The group sent back, the as yet not fully recovered, Eddy and Verrot to return the animals to Johnson's Ranch. On February 10th the reduced rescue party traveled on with heavy packs and no snowshoes. It was asking the impossible. The group made but six miles that day. The rescuers were rapidly exhausting themselves.

The next day the rescuers tried to make snowshoes, but the crude implements were useless. The snow stuck to the shoes making them cumbersome and heavy. It was back to walking through the knee-deep snow. On the February 12th, the snows began again. This was a bad sign, for the rescuers had yet to cross over the mountains.

Three of the party—Adolf Breuheim, M. D. Richey, and Jotham Curtis—gave up the rescue attempt. They could not be persuaded to go farther. Seven stalwarts continued the quest as the rest headed back. On the February 15th, the remaining rescuers

---

26   Further additions to the first relief expedition included Adolph Breuheim, William Coon, Jotham Curtis, William Eddy, M.D. Richey, George Tucker and Joseph Verrot.

were hit by a light snow and again forced to make snowshoes. The flagging party fought their way forward for three more days.

On February 18, 1847, the seven remaining rescuers made it through the pass! The rescuers were now on the same side of the mountain as the emigrants. But would there be anyone alive to rescue? By the evening they had worked their way to the vicinity of the Lake Camp. The rescuers called out to what looked to be an empty camp and were finally answered by a woman who, as if by magic, popped out of a snow bank and queried, "Are you men from California, or are you from heaven?"

> "Frid. 19th froze hard last night 7 men arrived from California yesterday evening with sam provision but left the greater part on the way to day clear & warm for this region some of the men are gone to day to Donnos Camp will start back Monday." (Diary of Patrick Breen)

The rescuers did what they could to ease the suffering. They distributed small amounts of food to the starving emigrants. The distance between the Alder Creek and Lake Camps made it difficult to provide help to all. However, the rescuers did reach the Alder Creek site and brought some of its occupants to the Lake Camp in preparation for taking them back to California.[27] It was clear to the rescuers that the emigrants were in desperate shape. The ravenously hungry unfortunates had been contemplating cannibalism if more help did not arrive soon.

The rescuers tried to locate the frozen carcasses of the missing cattle for food as the camp was down to consuming its last hides. Those who had no food and were relatively fit would be taken out. Those who were infirm, and those who would take care of their sick loved ones would remain behind. A total of twenty-two people remained at the Lake Camp.

Twenty-three made the desperate dash for escape. Fourteen of this group were under the age of sixteen, many mere infants. The rescuers had not materially helped the emigrants, but their presence did demonstrate that people could get through. The rescuers hoped to at least ease the suffering in the camps by

---

27 This group included Elitha Donner, George Donner Jr., Leanna Donner, Billy Hook, Noah James, and Mrs. Wolfinger

reducing the number of mouths to feed. They intended to bring out those who had the best chances of surviving several days of camping in the snow.

Another Walk to Salvation

> "With sorrowful hearts we traveled on, walking through the snow in single file. The men wearing snowshoes broke the way and we followed in the tracks. At night we lay down on the snow to sleep, to awake to find our clothing all frozen, even to our shoe strings." (Virginia Reed Murphy writing in 1891)

Glover's rescue party slowly struggled back up the mountain. Eight-year-old Patty Reed and her three-year-old brother, Thomas, could not make it. The two children were returned to the emigrant camp by Glover with a promise that he would return. At first the Breens refused to take in the two children; their food was stretched to the limits. Finally Glover talked them into caring for the children. Clearly despair was ruling the emigrant camp despite the arrival of help from Sutter's Fort.

The rescue party's charges were not doing well. The months of starvation and deteriorated conditioning caused by their confinement affected one after another of the party. Animals had partially devoured a cache of food upon which the rescuers had counted for sustaining them on the return journey. The next cache was at least four days walk. Four of the rescuers were dispatched ahead to find the cache and shuttle food back to the struggling party. The remainder continued forward, praying that the rescue did not turn into a death walk.

> "We had not proceeded far before the weather became intensely cold when we stopped for the night many of the party had their feet frozen. The next day our travel was slow, many in pain." (Virginia Reed Murphy writing in 1871)

John Denton collapsed and could go no farther. He was left behind in a warm quilt with a small portion of food and a blazing fire. No one expected him to live long. He had sufficient life left in him to write a poem, which was later found on his corpse. That night Ada Keseberg expired in her sleep. There were now nineteen of the rescued emigrants surviving and the prospects looked grim for the frostbitten skeletons who remained.

On the February 26th, two of the four rescuers who had been sent ahead to find the next cache, returned with food. Spirits were somewhat bolstered by this news. The next day the survivors spotted a group of men coming their way. It was another rescue party organized by Reed after his first attempt had been forced to turn back. Hope had returned.

Reed and the Second Rescue Party

Distressing News. by Capt. J. A. Sutter's launch which arrived here a few days since from Fort Sacramento—we received a letter from a friend at that place containing a most distressing account of the situation of the emigrants in the mountains, who were prevented from crossing them by the snow—and of a party of eleven who attempted to come into the valley on foot. The writer, who is well qualified to judge, is of the opinion that the whole party might have reached the California Valley before the first fall of snow, if the men had exerted themselves as they should have done. (Newspaper account published in the California Star on February 13, 1847)

As the above newspaper article suggested, the fate of the Donner Party was a matter of some concern to the residents of California. Already there was speculation of how such a thing could have happened. However, most of the concern was about what the people in California could do to end the tragedy.

James Reed, though concerned about his family, continued to indulge in the same wishful thinking that had him previously envision the Donner Party wintering on the western slopes of the mountains. He now believed the stranded emigrants had sufficient livestock to provide for them for several months to come. He was unaware as to the depth of desperation his family was suffering. The war interfered with Reed's continuing efforts to mount a rescue expedition and he was not aware that the first rescue expedition was on the way to the starving emigrants.

Reed convinced the people of San Jose to sign a petition urging a rescue expedition. On February 3rd he used the petition and a stirring speech at a rally in Yerba Buena where he managed to raise funds and volunteers. According to the *California Star* twenty brave men came forward. The expedition was ready to move out on February 6th. The expedition members thought themselves fortunate to include among their number eighty-three-year-old mountaineer Caleb Greenwood. He had come to the Rockies thirty-six years earlier with the Astorians.[28] Greenwood wagered that few of the flatlanders and sea lubbers in the expedition would return. Greenwood and Reed would take one party (the Second Rescue Party). Woodworth was to start by schooner with another party (the Third Rescue Party). Both left on February 7th, and help now traveled along several paths. William McCutcheon and William Eddy once again were on their way back into the jaws of death.

Reed's party was days behind the Glover party. Facing many of the same conditions that slowed Glover's First Rescue Party, Reed's men had a difficult trek. But the Second Rescue Party had many frontiersmen (including John Turner) who were well practiced in solving survival problems. Reed's group arrived in the nick of time. Without their opportune arrival, it is likely that Glover's relief expedition might have failed with enormous loss of life. The leaders of the various rescue expeditions established a relay of caches going up the mountain. If the animals left these precious stores alone and the snows did not hide them, there should be a steady chain of supplies on the walk to safety.

Camp Conditions Continue to Deteriorate

As the First Rescue Party and their twenty-three wards set off on their dash to safety, life for those left behind continued with the same grimness of the past months. Though a little food was left behind and there were far fewer people to feed now, the stocks of food were near the absolute end. Even those who had been well off at the start of the entrapment found themselves wondering how they would get by until more supplies could be brought in.

---

28   The Astorians were expedition of fur traders sponsored by John Jacob Astor, head of the American Fur Company. Greenwood was with the Stuart expedition of 1812 and did much to open the West to emigration.

Many of those remaining behind were already near death's door. They had survived to see loved ones and friends taken to safety, but for many of them the nightmare continued until death finished its icy work. In the meantime the emigrants each seemed to imagine that the others who remained behind had more food than they themselves did.

> *"Tuesd. 23 froze hard last night to day fine & thawey had the appearance of spring all but the deep snow wind S:S.E. shot Towser to day & dressed his flesh Mrs Graves came here this morning to borrow meat dog or ox they think I have meat to spare but I know to the Contrary they have plenty of hides I live principally on the same."* (Patrick Breen diary entry of February 23, 1847)

Morale evaporated after the Glover Rescue Party left the winter camp. Patrick Breen killed his dog, Towser, and the emigrants greedily consumed the little animal. An Indian passed by the camp but did not approach the emigrants. This visitor left a handful of roots for the starving strangers. The local wolves were busily digging up the bodies of the dead and gnawing upon them.

> *"Mrs. Murphy said here yesterday that thought she would commence on Milt. & eat him. I dont think that she has done so yet, it is distressing The Donnos told the California folks that they commence to eat the dead people 4 days ago, if they did not succeed that day or next in finding their cattle then under ten or twelve feet of snow & did not know the spot or near it, I suppose they have done so ere this time."* (Patrick Breen diary entry of February 26, 1847)

In the final days before the arrival of the Reed and Greenwood Rescue Party, Levinah Murphy butchered Milton Elliot's remains, which she and others consumed. This situation was mirrored in the Alder Creek Camp. As with the Forlorn Hope group roughly two months earlier, the dead would sustain the living. The awful decisions to choose survival over cultural prohibitions apparently were made independently at least twice and possibly three times. Once members of a local community or group had begun the process, it then became a series of individual choices for the adults as to what they would do so that they and their families could survive.

While Levinah was butchering Milton back in camp, Reed and his rescuers had found Glover's party.

> "I left camp early on a fine hard snow and proceeded about four miles when we met the poor unfortunate starved people, as I met them scattered along the snow trail I distributed Sweet bread that I had baked the two nights previous I give in small quantities, here I met Mrs. Reed and two children two still in the mountains I cannot describe the death like look they all had Bread Bread Bread Bread was the beging of every Child and grown person."
> (James Reed diary entry of February 26-27, 1847)

Reed had finally linked up with part of his family after a separation of many months. His wife and Virginia were still alive. Reed and his men passed out bread. They carried few provisions, but those following his seven-man advance group were well provided. He said good-byes to his wife and child again and moved on to rescue the remainder of his family.

With John Turner taking the point position, the Second Rescue Party pressed on at a rapid pace. They followed the beaten path even through the night, hardly stopping to rest. Compared with the previous rescue attempts this group of young, hardy lads seemed to fly. Shortly, three of the hardiest (Charles Stone, Charles Cady, and Nicholas Clark) went ahead of all the others. Cady, Stone, and Clark reached the stranded emigrants at the Lake Camp on March 1, 1847, and distributed what little food they brought with them. Reed was reunited with his two children later that day, as the remainder of the rescue party arrived.

The next day, Reed and several men from the Second Rescue Party visited the Alder Creek Camp. Conditions were very similar to those at the Lake Camp. Cady and Clark recounted finding Jean Baptiste on his way to the cook pot carrying the freshly butchered leg of Jacob Donner. Even after the arrival of the Second Rescue Party, children of the Jacob Donner camp continued to eat human flesh. George Donner was still in poor health, but Tamsen Donner and her three children seemed relatively healthy.

Reed planned to take those who were healthy enough to travel to safety. The plan called for leaving fellow rescuers Stone, Clark, and Cady with a week's worth of food to watch the remaining Donner Party members (including the healthy Tamsen Donner) until the next rescue party could come up. Reed determined to leave with seventeen of the emigrants.[29] He knew that members of Woodworth's Third Rescue Party could not be far behind. There was less of an air of emergency. Thoughts in both camps turned to caching valuables so they would be easy to recover in the spring.

> "I moaved camp and after a fatiguing day arrivd at the praire now Starved Camp at the head of the Juba it was made by the other Compy. who had passed in but a few days previous. here the men began to fail bing for several days on half allowance, or 1 1/2 pints of gruel or sizing per day. the sky look like snow and everything indicates a storm god forbid wood being got for the night & Bows for the beds of all, and night closing fast, the clouds still thicking terro. Terror, I feel a terrible foreboding but dare not communicate my mind to any, death to all if our provisions do not come in a day or two and a storm should fall on us, very cold, a great lamentation about the cold." (James Reed diary entry of March 5, 1847)

Walking out with Reed's Second Rescue Party

This return trip started out with a different atmosphere than the others. The emigrants thought to take prized possessions, such as a violin and money with them. They made painfully slow progress through the deep snows. Reed worried about another storm, but he could not hurry the walking skeletons any faster. Again food was running low. Reed sent three seasoned mountaineers (John Turner, Joseph Gendreau, and Matthew Dofar) ahead to the next cache to bring food back.

> "Still in camp the last of our provisions gone looking anxiously for our supplies none. My dreaded storm is now on us commed Snowing in the first part of the night and with the snow commed a perfect Hurricane in the night.

---

[29] This group included Isabella Breen, James Breen, John Breen, Margaret Breen, Patrick Breen Jr., Patrick Breen Sr., Peter Breen, Isaac Donner, Mary Donner, Elizabeth Graves Jr., Elizabeth Graves Sr., Franklin Graves Jr., Jonathan Graves, Nancy Graves, Solomon Hook, Patty Reed, and Thomas Reed.

> *A great crying with the children and with the parents praying crying and lamentations on acct of the cold and the dread of death from the Howling Storm."* (James Reed diary entry of March 6-7, 1847)

Before Turner, Gendreau, and Dofar could return with supplies, another storm hammered the rescue party. They were lucky to survive the night of freezing winds. All were exhausted and at the limits of endurance and still the storm pounded them all through the next day. That night the fire went out and only Herculean efforts by William McCutchen and Hiram Miller brought the flames back to life. They probably saved most of the lives of those in the group with this act. Still, success or failure of this rescue effort hung by a thread.

There was now no food. The storm continued another day and, on that third night, Isaac Donner perished. By the time the storm let up on the next day, several feet of snow had fallen. Those who were sufficiently fit moved on. Thirteen of the party, including the dead Isaac, remained behind. The Breens watched over the children. Mary Donner, who had burned her frostbitten foot during the storm, tried to leave but returned to the group after a short walk. Her burnt and frostbitten feet were not capable of taking her to safety.

> *"The second night Mr. Reed became snow blind and chilled through; he had overexerted himself in securing shelter for his party. Now there was only Mr. Miller and myself who were able to do anything; the rest of the men were disheartened, and would not use any exertion; in fact they gave up all hope, and in despair, some of them commenced praying. I d-d them, telling them it was not time to pray but to get up, stir themselves and get wood, for it was a matter of life and death to us in a few minutes. The fire was nearly out; the snow in falling off the trees had nearly extinguished it before discovered; it was only rekindled by exertion of Mr. Miller and myself. After we got the fire started I was so chilled that in getting warm I burned the back of my shirts, having four on me; only discovering the mishap by the scorching of my skin."* (William McCutchen writing in 1871)

Alder Creek Camp - Early March

At the Alder Creek Camp, after Reed left, Elizabeth Donner died. Nicholas Clark managed to kill a small bear, providing the camp with needed food. While he was chasing the bear after wounding it, Stone and Cady made arrangements with Tamsen Donner to take out her three children; Eliza, Frances, and Georgia. It is reputed that she paid them a tidy fortune of $500 for this task. The children said good-byes to their parents and were soon off, taking whatever valuables the family owned with them. Rather than take the children to safety, the duo dropped them off at the Murphy cabin and left. Here the children were tended by Mrs. Murphy and Mr. Keseburg. When Clark returned empty-handed to the Alder Creek Camp, the storm was beginning to gather in the sky. Soon the same storm that forced the Second Rescue Expedition to hold up was slamming into the Alder Creek and Lake Camps. Two days into the storm, Lewis Donner passed away. The numbing cold and hunger of the ordeal continued.

When the storm abated, Stone and Cady, carrying the Donner valuables, hurried out from the camps of death. They passed the shivering wards of the Second Rescue Party, now immobile, waiting under the care of Patrick Breen. Stone and Cady offered no assistance to this wretched, freezing band. The two rescuers caught up with Reed and helped his party on the final leg of their journey. Both Stone and Cady had frostbitten feet and were now moving as slowly as the rest of the party. They helped Reed carry out his suffering children.

Woodworth's Third Rescue Party Rescues the Rescuers

Turner, Gendreau, and Dofar, who had rushed ahead to bring back food to the foundering wards of the Second Rescue Party, found the first cache robbed by animals. They immediately pressed on to find the next cache, but were enveloped by the great storm. The mountaineers were completely unprepared for this. They managed to survive the storm, but were horribly frozen. The group found the plundered second cache and there remained some food at this location. Dofar managed to haul a little food back toward Reed before returning to his suffering friends. The rescuers were fortunate that after the storm William Eddy, William Foster, S. Woodworth, and five others from the Third Rescue Party had struck out to find Reed. The intrepid men of the Third Rescue Party found the three lost mountaineers first. They now knew that Reed and the wards of the Second Rescue Party could not be far. The rescuers of the third party were unaware that the Second Rescue Party had abandoned many of its wards and was itself on the verge of failing.

The Third Rescue Party men pressed on and slept within shouting distance of Reed and his group. Reed's surviving party found the food left by Dofar and with this sustenance was able to make it through another uncomfortable night in the snow.

As the Second and Third Rescue Parties came together, Reed's rescue was complete. The men of the Third Rescue Party learned that there were many left behind still shivering in the snow. The combined party moved back toward Johnson's Ranch. They needed to prepare far more carefully for the next rescue attempt. In the meantime the abandoned wards of the Second Rescue Party would have to wait and survive.

William Eddy and the Fourth Rescue Party

Once the combined rescue parties arrived at Johnson's Ranch, William Eddy, William Foster, and Charles Stone formed a new rescue party from the healthier members of the Second and Third Rescue Parties. This Fourth Rescue Party consisted of seven men.[30]
After outfitting themselves for the grueling trip back to the snowfields they started out with the purpose of saving the Breens and their charges, who were waiting where the Second Rescue Party had abandoned them. It was now March 11, 1847.

Woodward and the remnants of the Second and Third Rescue Parties began to take the survivors in hand to Sutter's Fort. There were so many with frozen limbs it took an extended time to get the walking skeletons fit for travel.

---

[30] The other members of this group were Hiram Miller, Howard Oakley, John Stark, and William Thompson.

On March 12th, the Fourth Rescue Party found the frozen body of John Denton. He had been left by the First Rescue Party wrapped in a quilt and with a fire burning nearby. The campfire soon expired and thereafter so did John. With Denton's frozen corpse the Fourth Rescue party discovered a scrap of paper upon which the freezing Denton had written a poem while waiting to die.

When the Fourth Rescue Party reached the stranded wards of the Second Rescue Party, they were reposing in a twenty-five foot deep cavern melted into the snow. The body of Mrs. Graves and two children had been butchered for food by the starving. Mrs. Graves' heart, liver, and breasts simmered in a pot as her baby cried nearby.

Three members of the Fourth Rescue Party set out for Johnson's Ranch with their charges on the morning of March 14th. It was difficult going but the little food provided by the rescuers was a help. Having strong men to help prod the group on made all the difference in their desperate hike for survival.

Eddy, Foster, and two others set out with all possible haste for the winter camp. The four men literally dashed for the stricken camp. What must have been their thoughts as they passed the partial corpses of those who had gone that way before? Seeing the sad state of the "rescued" emigrants, the two, were grievously worried about their children still in the winter camps.

They arrived too late. William Foster's son, George, died in Keseberg's bed. Mrs. Murphy accused Keseberg of murdering the boy. Who knows? Keseberg was quite capable of killing someone as he had done by abandoning old Mr. Hardcoop to die of exposure. The story about George Foster is very confused and all the witnesses were starved and probably suffering significant delusions. Eddy and Foster arrived but by that time the boy was gone.

James Eddy, the son of rescuer William also was dead. Eddy, was ready to kill Keseberg when the old "gentleman" mentioned eating James. Eddy apparently had forgotten his own cannibalistic adventures of a few weeks previous. However, calmer heads prevailed. The rescuers had their hands full in trying to figure out how to save the few emigrants who were left. There remained seven at the Lake Camp in need of rescue.

At the Alder Creek Camp, Elizabeth Donner had died. Nicholas Clark was lucky enough to kill a small bear so the camp had some food. Tamsen Donner was in remarkably good shape. George Donner was still very sickly. The rescuers stayed but a few hours and immediately took four children to the Lake Camp.[31] Nicholas Clark and John Baptiste were not to be found in either of the camps. These men had abandoned George Donner and set out to save themselves. However, this was not the last they were heard from.

Tamsen Donner saw her children off and returned to the tents on Alder Creek to tend her ailing husband. She refused to be taken out while he yet lived. Lewis Keseberg and Levinah Murphy stayed behind at the Lake Camp. The Fourth Rescue Party hastened to get out of the winter camps to safety. Unless there was a miracle, there was unlikely to be another rescue party until spring. Eddy and Foster must have thought those left behind would surely perish.

"When we reached the head of the lake, we overtook Nicholas Clark and John Baptiste who had deserted father in his tent and were hurrying toward the settlement. Our coming was a surprise to them, yet they were glad to join our party.

After our evening allowance of food we stowed snugly between blankets in a snow trench near the summit of the Sierras, but were so hungry that we could hardly get to sleep, even after being told that more food would do us harm" (Eliza Poor Donner Houghton writing in 1911).

The weather remained good and allowed the rescuers to bring out their charges. However, the warming trend actually discouraged most of the rescuers from considering joining additional rescue attempts by making the going extremely difficult.

---

[31] These were Eliza Donner, Frances Donner, Georgia Donner, and Simon Murphy.

The Fifth Rescue Party

There remained a few rescuers with enough pluck to go back for the last survivors. In late March Ned Coffeemeyer, Billy Graves, William Foster, John Rhodes, Joseph Foster, John Starks, and Reasin Tucker set out as the Fifth Rescue Party. This group hardly had set out and struggled through the heavy slush that choked Bear Valley, when the sight of a massive storm in the mountains ahead ended the rescue attempt. The focus of the various rescue parties switched to getting the survivors to Sutter's Fort. This was done over the next several weeks. The survivors filled up what little hospital space was available. The rescuers assumed that all of those who were left behind would perish and they mounted no further rescue attempts. Given the renewal of bad weather the four souls left behind might already be dead. They already had too much company.

The survivors who had been brought out to Johnson's Ranch still had a ways to go to safety. However, once at the ranch they could accustom themselves to eating increased quantities of food. Strength returned slowly.

The combined rescue parties and their wards next moved out to Mule Springs where it was expected to find horses that could carry them for the remainder of the journey to Sutter's Fort. They waited several days for the animals to arrive, all the while working on regaining their strength.

> "I found my little cousin Mary sitting on a blanket near Mr. Oakley, who had carried her thither, and who was gently trying to engage her thoughts. Her wan face was wet with tears, and her hands were clasped around her knee as she rocked from side to side in great pain. A large woolen stocking covered her swollen leg and frozen foot which had become numb and fallen into the fire one night at Starved Camp and been badly maimed before she awakened to feel the pain. I wanted to speak to her but when I saw how lonesome and ill she looked, something like pain choked off my words." (Eliza Poor Donner Houghton writing in 1911)

For most, the shock was over, but the horror of it was only just setting in. The survivors and rescuers alike sat up through many long nights entertaining the ghosts from that fateful winter.

> *"Oh, the balm and beauty of that early morning when Messrs. Eddy, Thompson, and Miller took us on horseback down the Sacramento Valley. Under the leafy trees and budding blossoms we road. Not rapidly, but steadily, we neared our journey's end." (Eliza Poor Donner Houghton writing in 1911)*

The Graves infant, Elizabeth, barely survived her rescue. She passed away some time after reaching Sutter's Fort. She was not the last to die.

> *"We kept watch of the cow-path by which we had reached the Fort for Elitha had told us that we might 'pretty soon see the relief coming.' She did not say, 'with father and mother;' but we did, and she replied. 'I hope so.'" (Eliza Poor Donner Houghton writing in 1911)*

The Donner children, though they did not know it yet, were orphans or soon to be such. They hoped and waited in vain for their parents to be brought in. As children often do in such circumstances, they lost themselves in exploring their new world. The fort, though a drab place to many, was a world of wonderful sights, smells, sounds and food.

> *"Many of the women were kind to us; gave us bread from their scant loaves not only because we were destitute but because they had grateful recollections of whose name we bore." (Eliza Poor Donner Houghton writing in 1911)*

However, the misfortunes of the children continued into the period after their rescue. "Charitable" souls in California swapped the fine silk dresses the girls had worn through their escape for second-hand clothing from their own daughters. Needless to say the fits were improper and the materials by no means matched the quality of the garments in which the girls had arrived.

Finally the news was given to the children that they would never see their parents again. Though it was not certain at the time, the rescuers did not believe that anyone would be found alive when the winter camps were next visited. Elitha Donner soon married. When she went off to live with her new husband, Perry McCoon, the Donner children were split up. Georgia and Eliza were placed in the care of the Brunners, an elderly Swiss couple. Frances lived with the Reed family.

The Forgotten Ones and the Fallon's Salvage Party

"A heavy storm came on in a few days after the last relief party left. Mrs. George Donner had remained with her sick husband in their camp, six or seven miles away. Mrs. Murphy lived about a week after we were left alone. When my provisions gave out, I remained four days before I could taste human flesh. There was no other resort—it was that or death." (Louis Keseberg in an 1879 interview)

The next expedition, led by mountaineer W. O. Fallon (also called Fellun) was to salvage equipment, possessions, and especially the caches of coins reputed to have been stored by the emigrants. On April 17, 1847, the party reached the camps. The Lake Camp was a scene of horror. Body parts were everywhere melting out of the snow. The bodies had been horribly mutilated. Fallon and his men had a start when they surprised three Indians who immediately ran away without a fight. The salvage party discovered a trail of an individual leading toward the Donner huts. Finding no one, the Fallon Party set about in its salvage work.

The next day three men resolved to follow the mysterious tracks in the snow. The rest remained to search for the missing coins. Those who stayed behind discovered the beef and horsemeat that had been buried in the snow and were still edible. They also found a kettle with human remains in it. As the snows melted, more treasures and horrors of the emigrants were revealed.

Following the tracks, the three searchers detached from the Fallon Salvage Party, found Louis Keseberg sleeping in a cabin amidst a scatter of human bones. The cooking pan contained human liver. Keseberg provided a story of the last month at the camp. He claimed that Mrs. Murphy died about a week after the last rescue party left. Tamsen Donner was reputed to have visited Keseberg after her husband died. If Keseberg is to be believed,

Tamsen apparently suffered from arctic hysteria, hypothermia, or some similar delusional episodes. When she died of exposure, Keseberg ate her remains with relish... "the best he had tasted." The presence of a kettle of blood led some to suspect Keseberg of murder. The rescuers began to torture Keseberg to reveal the secrets of the missing coins. With such an incentive he was willing to lead them to his cache of coins.

> "Imagine my astonishment upon their arrival to be greeted, not with a 'good morning' or a kind word, but with the gruff, insolent demand, 'Where is the Donner money?' I told them they ought to give me something to eat and I would tell them afterwards, but no, they insisted that I should tell them about the Donner's money. I asked them who they were, and where they came from, but they replied by threatening to kill me if I did not give up the money... they acted as though they were going to kill me... and finally I told them where they would find the silver buried, and gave them the gold. After I had done this, they showed me a document from Alcalde Sinclair, by which they were to receive a certain portion of all moneys and property which they rescued." (Louis Keseberg in an 1879 interview)

Keseberg at first unashamedly recounted his experiences as a cannibal. He had been doing a little salvage work of his own and had amassed as small fortune of $273 and many fine possessions of the dead emigrants. The salvage party confiscated all of these and proceeded with the search. Keseberg went back to his diet of human remains.

> "We asked Kiesberg why he did not use the meat of the bullock and horse instead of human flesh, he replied he had not seen them. We then told him we knew better, and asked him why the meat in the chair had not been consumed, he said, "Oh! it's too dry eating." the liver and lights[32] were a great deal better, and the brains made

---

32   When referring to "lights" it is not clear if Keseberg is using a 19th century vernacular for eyes or is referring to the lungs. Dishes made from lungs of sheep and/or cattle often are referred to as "lights." Take your pick for the actual meaning.

good soup!" (An excerpt of Fallon's journal printed in the California Star)

The Fallon party begrudgingly took Keseberg with them. He had difficulty in keeping up. Perhaps they wished he would perish on the trip back and join those upon whom he had feasted. On the return trip, Keseberg made a heartbreaking discovery. Keseberg related the following to Jacob Harlan.

"He was dragging himself along far behind the others, and stopped to rest at a place which had been used as a camping ground by one of the previous parties. He had with him some coffee, and filled his little coffee pot with snow, he set it on a fire which he had made, and sat waiting for the melted snow to boil. As he sat there he observed a little piece of calico which was uncovered by the snow. Half thoughtlessly, partly from idle curiosity, he took hold of the cloth and pulled it. It did not come easily, and he gave it a strong pull. A heavy substance came toward him. It was the body of his dead little girl, who had been taken to cross the mountains by the previous relief party, and had died and been buried in the snow which, having somewhat melted, thus uncovered part of her dress. This was the first information that he had received of his child's death." (Jacob W. Harlan writing in 1888)

The horrors already endured by Keseberg were almost unimaginable. Just when all appeared over, his rescuers tortured and shunned him. Now he had found the frozen body of a daughter, thought by him to have been safely in Sutter's Fort these past weeks. Some thought it the justice of an angry God. Some believed this is just another bit of bad luck in one of history's most incredible strings of bad luck. Keseberg was emotionally numb; something we recognize today as akin to "shell shock" or posttraumatic stress disorder. Things could have been worse. He, at least, survived to reflect on the events of 1846-1847. However, his ordeal had only begun.

The Fallon party returned to civilization on April 22, 1847. The last survivor of the Donner Party was in after almost seven months trapped in the snows. The telling of the tale fills volumes. It was now for journalists, archaeologists, adventurers, the military, and historians to track and document the remains (including the infamous cache of coins). Every passion play needs a villain and Keseberg was a convenient candidate. Rather than being the victim of tragic circumstances, he was vilified. After the *California Star* published an account of the Fallon party's "rescue" attempt Keseberg found himself a social outcast. Like a character in the Old Testament, members of the community figuratively stoned him (though not to death).

"Noble" Fallon added to the problems for the Donner children by arranging for the hasty auction of the family property not conveniently pocketed by the salvage party members. Half of the proceeds paid Fallon and his men and the remainder were proposed to be placed in the hands of a guardian for the raising of the children. Fifteen-year-old Elitha Donner already had married Perry McCoon. She left the remaining three Donner children in the fort to an uncertain future. She would return to them. But the family was shattered.

Aftermath

The survivors got on with their lives. As with any tale of death, suffering, weakness, heroes, heroines, and devils, there were protective spins regarding the events woven by the chroniclers. Take for example the 19th century America's most famous cannibal, Louis Keseberg. His initial, boastful acknowledgment of cannibalism, was replaced by the following,

> *"The flesh of starved beings contains little nutriment. It is like feeding straw to horses. I can not describe the unutterable repugnance with which I tasted the first mouthful of flesh. There is an instinct in our nature that revolts at the thought of touching, much less eating, a corpse. It makes my blood curdle to think of it! It has been told that I boasted of my shame—said that I enjoyed this horrid food, and that I remarked that human flesh was more palatable than California beef. This is a horrible, revolting falsehood. This food was never otherwise than loathsome, insipid, and disgusting. For nearly two months I was alone in that dismal cabin. No one*

knows what occurred but myself—no living being ever before was told of the occurrences. Life was a burden. The horrors of one day succeeded those of the preceding. Five of my companions died in my cabin, and their stark and ghastly bodies lay there day and night, seemingly gazing at me with their glazed and staring eyes. I was too weak to move them had I tried. The relief parties had not removed them. These parties had been hurried, too horror-striken at the sight, too fearful lest an hour's delay might cause them to share the same fate. I endured a thousand deaths. I am conversant in four different languages. I speak and write them with equal fluency; yet in all four I do not find words enough to express the horror I experienced during those two months, or what I still feel when memory reverts to the scene. Suicide would have been a relief, a happiness, a godsend! Many a time I had the muzzle of my pistol in my mouth and my finger on the trigger, but the faces of my helpless, dependant wife and child would rise up before me and my hand would fall powerless. I was not the cause of my misfortunes and God Almighty had provided me only this one horrible way for me to subsist." (Louis Keseberg in an 1879 interview)

Keseberg sued Edward Coffeemeyer, one of Keseberg's rescuers, for defamation of character. Coffeemeyer had asserted that Keseberg murdered Tamsen Donner. In response America's most famous cannibal sued to protect his reputation. The jury agreed with Keseberg, and the case was decided in his favor. There was no clear evidence that Tamsen Donner had been murdered. Perhaps a judgment on Keseberg's abandonment of Mr. Hardcoop to perish in the wild might have resulted in a different verdict. However, the admitted cannibal was not allowed to reap profit from his lawsuit. The jury's award of one dollar clearly indicated the low value placed on his "good name" and Keseberg was required to pay for the court costs.

Before we judge Keseberg too harshly, surviving members of the Donner Party considered him blameless in these matters. Perhaps those who had given into cannibalism themselves forgave Keseberg because they had difficulty forgiving themselves. In any case, they were not quick to add their voices to destroying what was left of the shattered Keseberg. All the other adults had a role in the turning out of Mr. Hardcoop by Keseberg, and the old man's death. Let he who is without sin… but then there were no sinless survivors of the Donner Party disaster as all, likely had become cannibals to survive.

The children grew up, married, and raised their own offspring. Life went on for the survivors. But it was never the same as each lived with the ghosts, dealt with the horrors, and reconciled the insanity of it all in his or her own fashion. For many survivors, it was decades before the restless hauntings within their souls quieted enough that they felt comfortable with writing about the ordeal for posterity. The infamy of the events of 1846-1847 followed the survivors throughout their lives. Mrs. Frank Lewis writing at the end of the First World War (November 23, 1918) still identified herself in her salutation as "Little Patty Reed, 1846, of the Reed-Donner Party." For at least one the notoriety of being a member of the Donner Party followed her to the grave as it was commemorated upon her tombstone.

Eliza and Georgia Donner entered St. Catherine's Convent to be educated. Upon entering the convent the Donner children were, according to custom of the place, asked to shed tears for five minutes. Georgia cried for ten minutes but Eliza indicated, "I don't wish to cry…"

Eliza was determined not to shed tears. She had suffered enough in her short life. Writing in later years, Eliza describes her encounter with the nun who was overseeing the Donner children's entry into the convent. It begins with the nun insisting that Eliza must shed tears, as was the custom for the convent's order.

> "'But', she insisted, 'you must shed a few entrance tears to--' Before she finished her sentence, and without thinking that if would be overreaching a stranger's privilege, I impulsively threw my arms around her neck, laid my cheek against hers, and whispered, 'Please don't make me cry'." (Eliza Poor Donner Houghton writing in 1911)

Eliza had cried enough for a lifetime and was admitted to the convent without further ceremony.

"I will now give you some good and friendly advice. Stay at home,—you are in a good place, where, if sick, you are not in danger of starving to death. It is a healthy country here when that is said all is said. Horses and cattle running wild on the commons are abundant. You can live without work if you are a complete rascal; for a rascal you must be to stand any chance at all. In the number of rogues this country exceeds I believe any other." (Mary Graves writing in 1847)

What If?

Much has been speculated about where the Donner party went astray. Would the party have heeded Edwin Bryant's letter to not attempt to try Hastings' proposed route if it had been delivered to them at Fort Bridger? What if they had listened to James Clyman's admonition, delivered near Fort Laramie, to stay on the main trail? Clyman actually had seen the territory the Hastings Cutoff traversed. Bryant's letter was based upon information from another person who had not seen the trail but was accurate about the difficulties ahead.

Would the party have pushed through the Sierra passes before the snows if their real leader, James Frazier Reed, had been allowed to stay with the party after he killed John Snyder? Did the party tarry too long just east of the Sierra passes resting five days for their final push? If the Indians didn't kill, steal, and injure so much stock would they have had sufficient food to last the winter? Should the party have wintered near the Great Salt Lake? What if the party had abandoned the "Hastings Cutoff" and returned to Fort Bridger? What if the party had followed the route through Weber Canyon and not been delayed carving their own route? What if the party had taken better care of their stock and not allowed them to become lost once they were trapped in the winter camp? There are a host of other "what-if" scenarios, which can be considered. However, the Donner party got to where they were by making their own decisions, taking risks, and living (or perishing) with the consequences. Like most people they made their decisions based upon what they knew and what they chose to believe were the likely outcomes. In their wildest nightmares they probably never envisioned the kinds of snows they faced in the Sierras.

Since the Donner Party missed getting across the mountains by a few days, one might pick any of the delays or stops as <u>the</u> days that cost the emigrants so dearly. However, one cannot indicate which of the delays was the most critical. Almost all emigrant trains faced delays. Clearly the several days lost while Reed met with Hastings are one of the best candidates for losing time to no-good purpose. Most of the other stopping days had an aspect of resting the stock and people for the next exertion. We need to look at the totality of days lost to the various delays, be they rounding up lost stock, recovering from an Indian attack, dealing with a murder, resting, scouting, recruiting stock, temporarily abandoning equipment, or repairing broken equipment. The emigrants frittered away weeks that could have been used to beat the storms (had they but known the date when the snows would lock them in).

When their plight became clear in the early fall, the emigrants made up much of the lost time through an incredible series of forced marches. However, it was too little, too late. They did not have a crystal ball to guide them, only their hopes, fears, and the tracks of wagons that had gone before them. Hopes and fears can easily blind one to what is really happening.

> *"At San Jose I met L.W. Hastings, whom I have mentioned as the man who advised us to leave the Fort Hall road and take the new cut-off recommended by him. I told him of our troubles, and the Reid and Donner calamaties, which resulted from following his advice. Of course he could say nothing but that he was very sorry, and that he meant well."* (Jacob W. Harlan writing in 1888 of a meeting with Lansford Hastings in 1846)

Murder... He Wrote

> *"I have often been accused of taking her life. Before my God, I swear this is untrue! Do you think a man would be such a miscreant, such a damnable fiend, such a caricature on humanity, as to kill this one lone woman?*

There were plenty of corpses lying around. He would only add one more corpse to the many!" (Louis Keseberg in an 1879 interview)

One aspect of the social interaction of the Donner party, which deserves consideration, is the high homicide rate.[33] James Reed murdered John Snyder. Lewis Keseberg was accused of killing Tamsen Donner and George Foster. It is clear that Keseberg's turning out of Mr. Hardcoop was simple murder as Mr. Hardcoop had no chance away from the wagon company. William Foster murdered Luis and Salvador. Joseph Reinhart and Augustus Spitzer murdered Wolfinger for his money. If all the suspected murders really were homicides, this would mean roughly eight percent of the main participants were murdered. Roughly twenty percent of all the deaths for this party were at the hands of their fellow travelers.

As many as four of the homicides may have been to provide food. The remaining three were related to other foibles of human nature, anger, greed, and selfishness. Three deaths by the hands of fellow emigrants for such a small party would be an extremely high number. Emigrant trains on the average could expect to lose between one out of every ten to twenty travelers. Almost all of these losses came from causes such as disease, old age, childbirth, and accidents. Death by murder of three or four percent of a wagon company was exceptional and usually related to skirmishes with groups of individuals and occurred within the context of a battle. A homicide rate of eight percent was unthinkable. The figure reflects how badly the social fabric of the group had been torn by month after month of privation.

It is surprising that the decision to resort to cannibalism apparently was reached independently by separate groups within the Donner Party. The "Forlorn Hope" group came up with the idea while separated from the main group huddling in the camps. The Forlorn Hope members were discussing the possibility of cannibalism as early as December 23rd, a mere week after leaving the camps. The inhabitants at the camps at the Lake and Alder Creek apparently decided upon the cannibalism option some time

---

[33] We do not consider in this tally the Native Americans outside of the party who were killed by the emigrants.

after the Forlorn Hope party had left. It was not until February that the subject of cannibalism was first recorded in the winter camps, curiously after the first of the rescue parties arrived. The stranded wards of the First Rescue Party likely were not aware of the cannibalism of the Forlorn Hope or that it began in the camps after the rescuers first left. However, it seems that the topic had been discussed in the camps at the time of their "rescue." It is not known if there might have been earlier discussions of cannibalizing the dead before Forlorn Hope left the camps.

Other emigrant companies had endured rough crossings without resorting to murder to provide food. The Utter (Otter) Party of 1860, another incident encompassing the themes of Indian attacks, starvation, and cannibalism, did not start murdering one another for food. All the bodies they ate died of starvation and exposure. Though the taboo about consuming human flesh gave into the need to avoid starvation, the Utter Party managed to maintain more of its social cohesion as relates to the taboo against murder. It causes one to ponder what made the Donner party take the other course.

Coping with starvation was an international problem. The year 1846 was the second year in the *An Gorta Mor* (the Great Hunger). With the failure of the Ireland's 1845 potato crop, came mass starvation and a tidal wave of emigration. Conservative estimates are that out of eight million inhabitants of Ireland roughly one million people perished between 1845 and 1849 because of the continuing crop failures. However, cannibalism on the scale of the Donner Party does not appear to have been the response to dealing with the ordeal of starvation. There were isolated instances of cannibalism in Ireland reported but only a handful given the vast numbers of people who were starving. Perhaps the isolation of the emigrants in the Sierras from church, law, and community had more to do with the choices made than researchers have been willing to credit.

The absence of civil/social authorities and the role this factor could have played in this tragedy deserves further examination. The 1856 Mormon Handcart disasters saw starving emigrants struggling through the snows and perishing from hunger by the score. Unlike the Donner Party, these handcart companies maintained strong social cohesion based upon church authority. The participants of the handcart disasters did not resort to cannibalism.

The absence of civil authority on the emigrant trails was typical in the middle 19th century. There was almost no law enforcement in the United States territory along the emigration corridor. Once out of Missouri there would be little civil authority encountered until well within California.

Mexican law enforcement was thinly spread in the hinterlands. In 1846, the start of the War with Mexico served to degrade what little law enforcement there had been. A curiosity of the times was that four individuals had been murdered with surviving witnesses present. Another had been murdered more secretively but the killers did not survive the journey. None of the surviving murderers did a day in jail or were even charged with a crime. Reed came the closest to feeling the stern hand of 19th century justice when Keseberg recommended lynching the murderer shortly after he stabbed Snyder to death. Instead Reed was exiled and there were no further repercussions for him. William Foster murdered Luis and Salvador but the racism of the time made it unlikely to charge a white man with murder when the victims were Indians.

The privations endured by the Donner Party could easily have strengthened the bonds of the group. Through the Great Salt Desert the party overcame one obstacle after another. One might think that their successes in these regards as well as their fear of the Indians could have forged them into a more cohesive group. However, the party took the opposite path and fractured into several small, occasionally hostile groups. After the Great Salt Desert the party fragmented into isolated groups often camping miles apart until something like the threat of being raided by Indians pushed them back together. Once stuck in the Sierras, and clearly in a situation that called for cooperation, the component groups of the Donner Party still camped apart. The Lake Camp had individuals camping roughly one-half mile apart and the Alder Creek Camp was separated by miles. As the snow piled up, it became increasingly difficult for the component groups to communicate with one another and working together was almost impossible.

Greed played a major role in the unfolding of events. Hastings wanted power and wealth. With the publication of his emigrant guide he hoped to attract settlers to California, where they would overthrow Mexican authorities and turn him into the leader of a new country. Bridger and Vasquez stood to gain from the opening of the Hastings Cutoff, leading to their support of the suitability of the route and perhaps not passing on Bryant's warning letter. Murder was committed for money within the Donner Party. Perhaps the fortune left to the Donners by Luke Halloran added to the friction between members of the wagon company. Many of the rescuers were only involved for the high pay offered. Fallon's party intended to salvage the property and find the missing fortunes supposedly abandoned at the camp. The lack of altruistic motives for Fallon and his men was evident in the torturing of Keseberg to find the missing coins.

Making sense of the mortality statistics for such a complex event is not easy. For example, Sarah Keyes died long before there was a Donner Party. Luke Halloran joined the group already on death's door. Thursday and his companion were officially brought into the party and then immediately left after robbing the emigrants. Antonio and Luis were never members of the party but were stranded with them and were murdered by them for food. If we exclude Sarah, Thursday, and Thursday's friend while including the latter three gentlemen in the totals, out of 89 participants only 48 (53.9%) survived.

It is difficult to find meaningful patterns in the mortality rates. Much has been made that in a group where 38% of the participants were female that 52% of the survivors were of that same gender. One might conclude that, all other things being equal women were 14% more likely to survive than would be expected by chance. However, all other things were not equal. The adult male population was considerably older than the female population. The group with the lowest survival rate was those people who were forty years of age or older.[34]

---

34 Survivors in this group were Patrick Breen (51), Margaret Breen (40), and James Reed (46). Those who died were Patrick Dolan (40), George Donner (60-62), Tamsen Donner (44), Jacob Donner (exact age unknown but older than 55), Elizabeth Donner (45), Franklin Graves, Sr. (57), Elizabeth Graves (45), Levinah Murphy (50), and Mr. Hardcoop (exact age unknown but certainly older than 40).

Excluding the same individuals mentioned above, there were thirteen individuals in this group, of whom three (23%) survived. The survivors of this group were only 33% female though the group was made up of 38% females.

So, why did so many of the younger men die as well? Those attempting to make sense of the statistics often ignore the effects of violent deaths and accidents upon the total. Four of the males were murdered, one suspected of being murdered, one died in a firearm accident, one joined the company almost dead. Three of the men were left alone to perish of exposure. It has been speculated that Tamsen Donner was murdered. Accordingly out of 55 male participants, as many as ten fatalities (18.2%) involved other factors than the privations of being trapped with little food. If one wants to exclude those murdered for food and the two abandoned because they were near death anyway the percentage shrinks to 10.9%. Conversely only one female out of 34 (2.9 %) is reputed to been made a fatality by other means. If we exclude all those who may have been helped along or abandoned to their deaths then 24% of the females died and 49% of the males perished as a result of the privations.

A social factor that does not receive consideration is that of gender roles. Victorian men were expected to risk their own lives to protect the women and children. For example, when William Foster was going somewhat crazy, desiring to murder and eat women in the Forlorn Hope Party, William Eddy risked his life to save them. When Foster wanted to shoot Luis and Salvador, Eddy protested but did not physically confront Foster as when the women were threatened. Eddy managed to save all five of the women, and the psychopathic Foster, when they all could go no further. Eddy found the energy to stagger forward until he found help to send back to the stricken and immobile traveling companions who were waiting to die. Had he failed in that effort there likely would have been more deaths among the women, perhaps losing all of them to Foster's violence or with the entire group perishing from exposure and starvation in the next cycle of storms.

Several of the men of the Donner Party such as Reed, McCutchen, Foster, and Eddy braved a return to the frozen hell of the mountains to rescue their friends and family members. Stanton returned from California with Salvador and Luis bringing supplies to the emigrants and all these men died trying to escape the entrapment. In Eddy's case it says much that he returned to the grimacing jaws of death so shortly after having just survived the Forlon Hope escape attempt by the thinnest of margins. In Victorian culture it was appropriate and almost expected for him to do so. Once brought to safety, none of the women returned to the horrors and dangers of the mountains. It was culturally inappropriate for them to take that role. They were expected to play a different part in the rescue, putting on a brave face and preparing the way for their families to return.

One of the great curiosities of the Donner Party story is why, when their food was gone and the way before them choked with nearly impassable snows didn't they retrace their path down to winter in the lower elevations in the snow-shadow of the mountains? Had they returned to the lowlands around Reno they likely would have found food and a much milder winter climate. The game in the mountains knew enough to use this strategy and if the emigrants were mainly flatlanders, the vaqueros clearly knew that as snow levels depress the game moves to the lower areas. When Eddy killed a deer during the Forlorn Hope escape he had just reached the edge of the snow line, where one might expect to have a chance of finding game. Dispatching well-armed hunting parties to bring food from the lowlands back to the camps was a fair option but the move of the entire company closer to areas likely to contain game was a better strategy.

Once in the fertile valleys the emigrants could have licked their wounds and recruited their strength for the spring. Such a move took them further from their destination and rescue but put them into a situation where rescue was no longer a desperate necessity.

There is no one person to blame here, except perhaps Lansford W. Hastings, promoter of a fraudulent shorter route to California. However, one must remember that Hastings was with the Harlan-Young Party and shared their privations. They luckily had a substantial head start on the Donner Party and did not expend themselves carving out the Echo Canyon road. The Harlan-Young Party was through the passes shortly before the snows sealed the route. Had the snows come earlier, the Donner Party might have found itself with Hastings, the Harlan-Young Party, and Hoppe Parties for company. Members of the Donner Party were not unanimous in whether to blame Hastings.

The Donner Party had been warned by mountaineer James Clyman that the Hastings Cutoff was unsuitable for wagons. Early on in the process, they had ample proof that Hasting was inaccurate and that the Clyman warning was true. One would think that after having to blaze a road into the Valley of the Great Salt Lake, the futility of trying to complete the route so late in the season would have sunk in. If they had not been mislead as to the remaining distance to California they might have considered staying in the Valley of the Great Salt Lake or even going back to Fort Bridger for the winter. Once across the Great Salt Desert, this option became less viable.

If the Donner Party's experiences were the subject of a modern-style incident debriefing, the issue of the failure of leadership clearly would rise to the top as turning a bad situation into a mass casualties event several months in duration. When the Donner Party exiled James Reed, no one stepped up to become the real leader of the company. Reed had seen the company through the Echo Canyon and Great Salt Desert tribulations and, by the time he was exiled, the group had increased its pace to an astounding twenty miles per day. He had even dispatched two riders to bring food back to the emigrants. George Donner seems to have been a nice person but clearly was not leadership material. With Reed gone, overall progress slowed and the wagon train splintered into several small groups, often camping miles apart. The smaller groups were more inviting targets to be raided and the losses of livestock to arrow wounds skyrocketed after the leadership of the company was exiled. The murder of Snyder by Reed turned from an isolated instance to an eventual murder spree, further deteriorating the social structure of the collective company.

Reed had his faults as a leader. Before his exile for murder he managed the unfortunate emigrants from one misadventure to another. Despite plenty of reasons to stop following Hastings, Reed kept the wagon company following one bad set of directions after another. In many respects it was his leadership that kept the wagon company set on the path that led to such sorrows. When his skills at keeping the emigrants moving forward as a group were eliminated due to his exile, the company shattered. By that time the emigrants had few options, push on or hold up somewhere for the winter.

The Donner Party, as the last train on the trail that year, harvested all the bad will the previous wagon companies had sewn among the local tribes. Emigrants too often had a shoot-first mentality when dealing with Native Americans. Additionally there were cultural barriers that stood in the way of good relations. For example, the local Native American cultures readily shared resources. The coming of so many emigrants with such wealth in livestock and possessions promised a jubilee if the emigrants were a fraction as generous as were the Native Americans. Instead the tribesmen found people who were, by tribal standards and customs, stingy. Such attitudes made the local tribes less willing to be friendly hosts to these strange trespassers.

The Donner Party was harassed by their Indian "hosts" more than the previous trains. Such a situation alone called for strong leadership to bring the emigrants through. The splintered segments of the Donner Party became easy targets for being robbed or attacked. When there were actual hostilities with Indians the emigrants gathered closer together but never established a unified leadership that lasted past the danger. The lack of a common identity and recognition that they were in this survival situation together assured that the company was unable to act with the common purpose necessary to reduce the loss of life.

When the emigrants were trapped on the wrong side of the mountains, they scattered themselves into many small camps. With strong leadership, the resources they possessed at the time of their entrapment might have been husbanded and protected sufficiently to get the group through the winter. The loss of their remaining livestock, because they had been allowed to wander free during a blizzard, was a monstrous mistake that doomed many of the company to die slow and horrible deaths. The animals were life itself and warranted being corralled and guarded, yet there was no leadership to assure these measures were carried out. The real leader of the group was on the other side of the mountain trying to arrange for food to reach the emigrants but his absence from the trapped camps was far more of a loss to the group than the help he later mustered.

Firm leadership likely would have recognized the depth of the dangers in their survival situation at an earlier time and focused efforts on a unified survival plan rather the many poorly conceived and executed escape attempts by the able-bodied members, the very people necessary to do the toil necessary to keep the group alive. The Donner Party not only sent it's leadership to the wrong side of the mountain, it exhausted its strength by allowing the most able-bodied among them to perish from exposure and fatigue themselves in escape attempts.

However, the Donner party proved to be incredibly stubborn, some would say driven. That quality served the group well in assuring that there were survivors despite all of the poor decisions and poorer luck. However, it was the same quality that made the depth of their misfortunes possible. How many times did the surviving adults lie in the comfort of a quiet, warm room listening to the wind blow punctuated by the coughing of the children and wonder,

"What if we had only . . . ?"

John Denton's Last Poem — Found Upon his Corpse

"O! after many roving years,
How sweet it is to come
Back to the dwelling-place of youth,
Our first and dearest home;
To turn away our wearied eyes
From proud ambition's towers,
And wander in those summer fields,
The scenes of boyhood hours.

But I am changed since last I gazed
Upon that tranquil scene,
And sat beneath the old witch elm
That shades the village green;
And watched my boat upon the brook-
It was a regal galley-
And sighed not for a joy on earth,
Beyond that happy valley.

I wish I could once more recall
That bright and blissful joy,
And summon to my weary heart
The feelings of a boy.
But now on scenes of past delight
I look, and feel no pleasure,
As misers on the bed of death
Gaze coldly on their treasure."

Words of Wisdom From a Rescued Child

> "O Mary I hav not rote you half of the truble we have had but I have rote you anuf to let you now that you dont now what truble is but thank god we have all got throw and the onely family that did not eat human flesh we have left everything but I dont cair for that we have got throw with our lives but Dont let this letter dishaten anybody never take no cutofs and hury along as fast as you can"

Letter of Virginia Reed to her cousin shortly after her rescue — May 16, 1847 *(Illinois Gazette)*

Reflection

"God has been our guide; not through snows and THE starvation, but through the bloodshed of war.

Greetings with all kindest wishes to you and each member of the Donner Parlor of Truckee. I trust we shall meet again, clasp hands of friendship, and be glad.

I am your old Pioneer friend.

MRS. FRANK LEWIS
Little Patty Reed, 1846, of the Reed-Donner Party."

(Patty Reed writing at the end of World War I in a letter dated November 23, 1918.)

Recipes

Mr. Keseberg, if I didn't know better I'd think you were trying to smoke me and not the sausage.

Gruel

Water/Milk	one pint
Corn Meal	4 Tablespoons
Salt	or salt pork
Loaf Sugar	to taste
Nutmeg	1/4 Teaspoon
Raisins	1 Tablespoon

Boil water in skillet. Add corn meal, nutmeg, and raisins. Stir while boiling for ten minutes. Add salt and sugar to taste. Serve piping hot.

Those with a sweet tooth may wish to throw in a little cinnamon. Those with adventurous palates may wish to add a little ginger root.

Note: Most of us view gruel as a "punishment food." That is... we give that stuff to prisoners or bad children. However, in the 19th century gruel was a simple and flavorful dish. Many times those who were ill would require a less rich diet. A good gruel is easily digestible and hence sick individuals often were prescribed gruel. Gruels often were well seasoned. Gruel will not be one of those dishes one naturally gravitates towards when hunger pangs are being felt. ("Gee, I sure could go for a good bowl of gruel!")

Lumpy Dicks

Milk/Water	2 cups
Flour	up to 2 cups
Sugar	2 tablespoons
Cinnamon	2 tablespoons

Bring milk/water to a boil. Add flour until the dish takes upon the consistency of mush. Stir slowly and boil for five minutes. Top with sugar and cinnamon.

Note: This dish is another simple, but flavorful, meal. The name creates a lot of improper images. This was a favorite of many emigrants. This particular recipe will serve two.

Corn Dodgers

Cornmeal	2 cups
Bacon Grease	1/2 cup
Scalded Milk	1 cup
Baking Soda	2 teaspoons
Salt	1/3 teaspoon

Scald milk in a sauce pan. Stir in corn meal, baking soda, and salt. The mixture should form a moderately loose dough. Shape into eight to ten oblong dough balls (dodgers). Heat bacon in frying pan over hot coals. Place the dough balls in the hot grease and fry until both sides are brown. Be careful not to overcook!

Note: This is a simple, travelers' dish. It uses the excess bacon grease to make a tasty treat, which the traveler can snack on between cooked meals.

Slapjacks, Flapjacks, Pancakes, Flat Jacks

Flour or Buckwheat Flour	2 cups
Milk	1 cup
Water	As needed
Eggs	1
Baking soda	1/2 teaspoon
Cinnamon	to taste
Sugar	to taste

This recipe is best if the pan used to fry bacon is used with the bacon grease still in it. Otherwise use lard or butter to coat the pan. Mix the flour, milk, sugar, and cinnamon. Add sufficient water to make a loose batter. Smaller cakes (up to four inches in diameter) are easier to cook than larger cakes. Cook over low coals in a hot, greased pan. The more grease the better. Flip the flapjacks as the bottom browns. (Hint... the first side is done when the middle of the flapjack has filled with bubbles. Time the second side to match the cooking time of the first side.)

Some may wish to substitute soured milk for the milk and water to make an especially sharp taste. Some might wish to substitute buckwheat flour for wheat flour. Some might wish to add flavor by pulverizing hard bread and adding it to the flour. A little butter in the batter is always a nice touch.

Note: What would breakfast in the outdoors be without flap jacks? This is a basic recipe which despite its simplicity yields almost foolproof good results. Well... maybe "foolproof" is a little strong. Just remember to cook over glowing coals... not flames.

Johnny Cake, Journey Cake, Hoe Cake

Corn Meal	6 cups (Some use rice instead)
Flour	1 cup
Water	As needed
Milk	2 cups
Salt	1 teaspoon
Molasses	3 teaspoons
Lard	2 tablespoons

Scald the milk in a saucepan. Add lard and let melt. Add corn meal, salt, and four. Stir in water until a stiff batter results. Add molasses and mix in. Shape cakes into roughly three-inch diameter disks no thicker than 1/2 inch. Cook over low coals in a hot, greased pan. This recipe tastes best when left over bacon grease is used to fry the cake. Fry until cooked throughout.

Some may wish to substitute baking in a greased dutch oven for frying.

Note: Journey-cakes were very popular in the 19th century. They are an example of a filling, easy-to-make snack which can make the long hours of walking seem shorter. They also have the side effect of reducing one's problems with diarrhea. If you have ever worn clothing from the period you will understand how difficult it is to rapidly strip down sufficiently to take care of nature's functions. A diet with such food is a blessing as it gives one more control over their own nature. Definitely a good thing according to Victorian culture!

On the other hand if constipation is your problem... eat more things with pepper sauces in them.

Son of a Sea Dog, Hish and Hash, or Skileegallee

Biscuits (Hardtack)	two
Bacon Grease	1 cup
Peppersauce	optional
Water	As needed

Soak two biscuits in water until soft enough to crumble. Add to hot bacon grease and cook until the entire mixture is a similar consistency and very hot. The bold cook can add peppersauce to taste.

Canned tomatoes and hard cheese can be added for a zesty repast.

Note: This is a tasty meal that can be made with leftover grease and hard bread. The dish was popular among the military and civilians alike. There must be over a dozen names for this same dish. Many have trouble eating this because the meal looks unappetizing. Be adventurous and trust your nose and taste-buds.

Antelope Pudding

Antelope Meat	2 pounds
Potatoes	2 pounds
Milk	2 cups
Flour	2 cups
Salt	1 tablespoon
Peppercorns	1 tablespoon, crushed
Lard	4 tablespoons
Cinnamon	3 teaspoons
Loaf Sugar	4 tablespoons
Apples	2 pounds
Water	As needed

Make a crust first by mashing potatoes in milk and salt. Add flour and lard to the mixture until a dough results. The dough is spread thin across the bottom of a Dutch oven or deep pie pan. The antelope meat is chopped into stew meat portions. Place a layer of the chopped meat in the bottom of the pan with just enough water to partially cover the meat. Add peppercorns and place a layer of crust on top. Slice the apples into small sections similar in size to the stewed meat. Place the sliced apples on the second layer of crust. Add loaf sugar and cinnamon and cover with another layer of crust dough. Seal the crust on top of the pan and place over moderate coals for thirty to forty minutes.

Some may improve the flavor by adding lemon juice to the apples or a layer of canned peaches.

Note: Meat puddings were very popular in the 19th century. The recipe above can be used for a variety of meats besides antelope. Antelope was another food source which could be gathered along the trail. Probably antelope became a staple somewhere east of Fort Bridger, where the buffalo sometimes were scarcer.

The average antelope does not provide much meat but they are an easy animal to hunt, even for inexperienced emigrants. Emigrant guides suggest that if a piece of cloth is hung from a stick and allowed to flap in the wind the curious antelope will come in close to see what the flap is about. This makes them easy prey. Many an emigrant's supper included antelope meat. Antelope meat is considered by many to be "gamey." It is difficult to prepare properly for diners used to beef. Many claim that antelope is fit only to make jerky or sausage. Baking the meat into a pudding should mask much of the sage flavor, which some find distasteful.

Arrowroot Pudding

Arrowroot	1 Tablespoon
Water	see below for amount
Milk	1 cup
Nutmeg	to taste
Cinnamon	to taste

Mix arrowroot and water in sufficient quantity to make a lump-free paste. Boil milk and slowly add the arrowroot paste. Simmer until the mixture thickens and becomes somewhat gelatenous. Add nutmeg or cinnamon. This recipe makes a single serving

Note: Puddings were very popular with our 19th century ancestors. This recipe creates a light pudding which might be used to feed the sick or just those who needed something light and flavorful. It is very tasty and can be spread over bread or biscuits for a more filling meal.

(Recipe courtesy of Jerri Spellman)

Rice Pudding

Rice	1 pint
Milk	1 quart
Eggs	5
Loaf Sugar	1/4 cup
Salt	1 teaspoon
Nutmeg	1/2 teaspoon

Boil milk and rice together over low to moderate coals for five minutes. Add eggs, sugar, and salt. Allow to come to a boil and then transfer to a greased pan or Dutch oven. Sprinkle ground nutmeg over the top of the pudding and cover. Bake over medium coals for twenty minutes.

Note: This recipe makes for a very nice and flavorful pudding. Puddings were a very popular component of the 19th century table and there was a rich variety of puddings available.

Brain Stew

Brains	roughly two pounds
Milk	one pint
Butter	1/16 pound
Vinegar	one tablespoon
Salt	to taste
Peppercorns	to taste

Brains need to be soaked in salt water until they stop giving off a bloody brine. When brains are ready, put them in kettle and cover completely with water. As the water starts to boil add milk and butter. Add salt and ground peppercorns (black pepper) to suit taste. The mixture should boil for ten to twelve minutes. When cooked place on serving dish and add vinegar. You may want to put some Walnut Catsup on the serving dish as a substitute for the vinegar.

Note: The average 19th century person ate a variety of organs on a regular basis. Brain stew was a favored dish. When the Fallon Salvage Party found Lewis Keseberg, he was in the process of preparing a brain stew and Tamsen Donner was missing. It does give one pause to wonder. The only court case regarding this matter was a defamation of character suit by Keseberg against one of his rescuers. The jury found no direct evidence that Keseberg had murdered Tamsen Donner. However, it was abundantly clear that Keseberg was a cannibal and even went so far as to praise the quality of the meals he had made from Tamsen Donner.

Buffalo Stew

Buffalo Roast	3-4 pounds
Salt Pork	1/4 pound
Onions	2
Carrots	4
Potatoes	6
Garlic	1 clove
Rosemary	1/4 teaspoon
Sweet Basil	1/2 teaspoon
Salt	1 tablespoon
Pepper	1 tablespoon
Water	2 quarts

Cut meat into stew-sized portions. Dice the salt pork and put in a large kettle over medium coals. As the salt pork cooks, it will render grease. As this occurs, add all the buffalo meat to the kettle and brown the outside. When the meat is browned, add water to the kettle and bring to a boil for fifteen minutes. Reduce the heat from the coals to a low heat. Dice onions, carrots, and garlic and add to the kettle. Add salt, pepper, sweet basil, and rosemary. Quarter potatoes and add to the kettle. Cover the pot and allow to simmer for two to three hours. Serve piping hot.

The adventurous might wish to pour some pepper sauce or ground mustard seed into the mixture. If the meat is too tough, allow it to simmer between one and two hours until it becomes flaky.

Note: Buffalo would have been available to the emigrants along much of the trail to California. Buffalo does not have the fat marbling one would expect from beef and tends to taste a bit more "gamey" than beef. Most emigrants who expressed an opinion thought the taste of buffalo was quite pleasing. Shooting buffalo along the way allowed the emigrants to save their cattle for the trip and otherwise stretch their stores of food. When roasting/frying buffalo care must be taken to avoid overcooking. This recipe allows one to savor the flavor of buffalo without having to learn through trial-and-error the proper roasting of this kind of meat. This recipe can be converted to beef or horse with pleasing results.

Mutton Soup

Mutton	2 pounds
Water	2 quarts
Onions	2
Carrots	1
Barley	1/4 cup
Ramps/Leeks/Scallions	3
Celery	1/2 cup
Peppercorns	1 teaspoon, unground
Salt	2 teaspoons
Parsley	1 tablespoon
Sweet Basil	1 tablespoon

The mutton should be separated from all bones and gristle. The meat should be cut into thumb-sized portions. The amount of fat which is acceptable to leave is a personal choice. Place mutton and water in large pot and bring to a boil. Dice the onions, celery, carrots, ramps/leeks/scallions and add to the pot. Add all the other ingredients. Some may wish to skim off the fatty foam. Reduce the heat and simmer with the lid partially uncovered for ninety minutes. Don't forget to stir the pot regularly. The soup should be served piping hot.

Truly bold cooks may add pepper sauce, green peppers, or chili peppers to taste.

Note: Our ancestors used to eat a lot more mutton than we do. Those who do not like the mutton to taste "like sheep" will find that this recipe mellows the flavor quite well. The recipe also works using Mountain Sheep meat.

Potato Soup

Potatoes	3 pounds
Rice	1 cup
Salt	2 tablespoons
Peppercorns	1 tablespoon
Milk	1 cup
Water	1 gallon
Arrowroot	2 tablespoons
Soup Bone	

Slice potatoes very thin and add to water in a large pot or kettle. Put vessel over low coals. Bring to a boil and add rice, salt, crushed peppercorns, milk, and a large soup bone. The soup bone can be from a moose, elk, deer, beef, buffalo, or sheep. Boil for one-half hour. Reduce heat and simmer for another fifteen minutes. Serve hot.

Some might wish to substitute millet or barley for the cup of rice. Soured milk will make for a sharper tasting soup. Some might wish to substitute salt pork for the soup bone. This is a good soup base and can be poured over bread (hard or soft) for a flavorful treat.
Note: Soups were very popular because they allowed one to feed a lot of people with limited supplies. Soups and broths were also used extensively for feeding the sick.

Ox Tail Soup

Oxtail	2.5 pounds
Onion	1
Garlic	1 clove
Celery	2 cups
Apple Vinegar	½ cup
Carrots	1 pound
Potatoes	3 pounds
Shucked corn	2 cups
Green peas	1/2 cup
Green beans	1/2 cup
Tomato Puree	1 pint
Black Pepper	to taste
Salt	to taste
Rosemary Spears	to taste
Bay Leaves	2
Olive oil	4 tablespoons
Worcestershire Sauce	to taste

Water (sufficient to completely cover the other ingredients)

Chop the Oxtail meat into stew sized pieces. Dice the celery, carrots and onion and sauté the onion in the olive oil until caramelized. Cut the potatoes into pieces double the size of the oxtail meat. Chop the garlic very fine.

Dip the oxtail meat in the apple cider vinegar and sprinkle salt, pepper, and Worcestershire sauce over the stew meat. Immediately sear the exterior of the oxtail meat over a high temperature fire until the exterior is lightly browned (this usually takes about four minutes).

Over moderate heat place water, browned oxtail meat, caramelized onion, celery, carrots, potatoes, corn, peas, green beans, tomato puree, garlic and spices into a large covered pot. Bring the mixture to a rapid boil and allow to boil for thirty minutes. Reduce the heat to a temperature sufficient to simmer the mixture. Simmer overnight (a minimum of six hours but no more than ten hours). Be sure to make sure you stir the pot and sample as you go so you can adjust spices.

You can make bold with this recipe by adding chili powder, cilantro, and/or hot sauce to taste. Serve piping hot and have a wonderful holiday.

Irish Potato Salad

Irish Potatoes	one dozen
Bacon Grease	5 tablespoons
Vinegar	5 tablespoons
Parsley	1 Teaspoon
Salt	to taste
Peppercorns	to taste

Boil the Irish potatoes until soft. When cool cut the potatoes into small pieces. Place in large bowl or pot. Stir in bacon grease and vinegar. Chop the parsley and add to the mixture. Add salt and ground peppercorns to taste.

Note: For the 19th century individual Irish potatoes were what we now call white potatoes. Yams (sweet potatoes) were also referred to as potatoes. The Irish designation is accurate to the period and allowed one to distinguish these from yams.

Bacon and Rice

Bacon	1/2 pound [It wasn't pre-sliced in those days.]
Rice	2 1/2 cups
Water	3 1/2 cups
Salt	1 Tablespoon
Peppercorns	1/2 teaspoon, crushed
Tomatoes	canned, 12 ounces
Peppersauce	to taste

Slice bacon into portions roughly 1/4 inch thick. Sauté bacon in a saucepan until slightly brown. Add water and bring to a boil. Add rice and boil until soft. Add seasoning and tomatoes and slowly bring to a boil. Drain off excess water and simmer until thick. Total cooking time usually is under thirty minutes.

Note: This is an excellent meal which is nutritious and filling. At the end of a hard day on the trail this could be put together with little fuss and is most pleasing to the palate. For those on the schedule of emigrants this would make a fine "nooning" meal, when the train is stopped for a mid-day siesta.

Baked Beans

Beans	two pounds
Salt Pork	one pound
Molasses	one half pound
Onion	one-half
Mustard Seed	one teaspoon
Water	as needed

Soak the beans for twenty-four hours prior to cooking. Drain the water off and add fresh water. Place over medium coals and bring to a boil. Reduce temperature to a simmer and add salt pork, molasses, and mustard. Sauté one half an onion in bacon grease or oil. When golden brown add to the bean pot. After simmering an hour, transfer the beans to a bean pot and place covered pot in a medium oven for roughly nine hours. Then uncover pot and place back in oven allowing the top to brown into a crust. Once the beans are baked they can be used in a wide variety of recipes.

Some may wish to sweeten the pot by adding sugar. Others may wish to sharpen the flavor by adding a condiment such as walnut catsup.

Note: Beans are considered a standard of western fair. This is a very basic bean recipe and works for a variety of beans. The long cooking time makes beans a dish for a period of rest. Otherwise place the beans to soak in a small cask, covered bucket, or canning jar.

Walnut Catsup

Walnuts	50, crushed
Vinegar	2 quarts
Scallions/Ramps/Leeks	1 pint, diced
Salt	1 tablespoon
Peppercorns	1/4 cup
Garlic	1 cup
Allspice	1/4 cup
Ginger	1 teaspoon
Cloves	to taste
Horseradish	2 Tablespoons
Mustard Seeds	1/2 cup
Mace	4 Tablespoons
Nutmeg	2 Tablespoons
Sugar	2 Tablespoons

Mix all the above ingredients well. Place in a jug and cork tightly. Set the jug in the sun between five and seven days. Be sure to shake the jug each day. Just keeping it hanging from the back of a moving wagon during the day should more than suffice. At the end of this period place mixture in a pot and boil well. When cool, strain the mixture and bottle in well-sealed containers.

This is a fine, flavorful condiment for meats. The condiment comes out a deep violet color. It takes a little getting used to seeing a purple sauce on one's steak but it has a fine flavor. By the way... for those who are interested in writing to others about their meals the liquor from the catsup is a fine, indelible ink. Yes, it will stain your tongue, dishes, and anything else it comes into contact with. (That should be sufficient warning as to what it will do to your kitchen should it be spilled.)

Note: Catsups of many varities were extremely popular in the 19th century.

Rabbit

Rabbit Meat	from one rabbit, cut into small bits
Wheat Flour or	
Buckwheat Flour	1 cup
Onion	1 diced
Lemon Juice	3 tablespoons
Animal Fat	
Salt	1 teaspoon
Peppercorns	crushed, to taste
Rosemary	to taste

Take the cut up meat, dip in the lemon juice and roll in a mixture of flour and spices. Put the meat in a pan containing the animal fat and onions. Sauté over a medium-hot set of coals until the meat is thoroughly cooked.

Those who wish to stretch the meal can add rice and vegetables.

Note: Rabbit can be an excellent meat dish. No, it doesn't taste like chicken! The above recipe makes for a tasty, light meal.

Venison

Venison Roast	roughly 2-3 pounds
Bacon	1/4 pound
Flour	3/4 cup
Onion	1
Celery	1/4 cup
Peppercorns	1/2 teaspoon
Salt	1/2 teaspoon
Water	3 cups

After slicing, place the bacon in a dutch oven over a medium heat and melt out a quantity of the bacon grease. Cover the venison with flour and rub into the meat as much as possible. Add 1 & 1/2 cups of water to the hot oven and place the roast in the oven until browned. This will involve turning the roast over. While roast is browning dice the onion and celery. Add to oven when outer portions of the roast have browned. Add all additional spices and 1 & 1/2 cups of water. When water has come to boil, reduce heat to a simmer and cover the pot. Allow to simmer for at least one hour. Cooking time will vary due to heat of coals and size of cut of meat.

Note: Venison would have been available almost throughout the entire trip. When prepared right venison has a very tender and flavorful meat.

Scrapple

Salt Pork	2 pounds
Beef or Pork Liver	1 pound
Flour	3 1/2 cups
Corn Meal	2 1/2 cups
Peppercorns	1/2 teaspoon
Salt	1/4 teaspoon
Sage	1/4 teaspoon
Water	3 quarts

Place water, salt pork, and liver in large pot over hot coals. Boil until the salt pork is tender. Remove the salt pork and the liver and grind it. Return the ground liver and salt pork to the pot and add flour, corn meal, and seasonings. Boil for roughly one hour making sure to stir the mixture frequently and well. Pour the mixture into small pans. When cooled, slice the mixture. Place it in a pan which contains bacon grease or lard and fry until crisp on both sides.

Note: This is a great way to make liver more palatable for those who don't like to eat organs. This is a good snack food. Modern liver afficionados might wish to smother the meat in sautéed onions.

Mince Meat

Leftover Meat   2 cups
Leftover Vegetables   2 cups
Apples   4
Sage   1/8 teaspoon
Meat Drippings or Gravy
Soft Bread

Chop leftover meat and vegetables very fine. Place in pan with meat drippings or gravy and heat over low coals. Slice apples and lightly brown in a frying pan. Add apples to mixture and sprinkle sage over the top. When warm the mixture is placed on toasted soft bread with additional gravy or warm meat drippings to increase flavor.

Some may wish to add pepper sauce.

Note: Mince(d) meat generally was considered a low-quality food. It is intended to make the best use of leftover meat and vegetables. However, it can be an extremely tasty treat. The mince(d) meat can be used in puddings, pies, and muffins. The dish is not for the weak of heart.

Buffalo Tongue

Buffalo Tongue	1
Onion	1
Cloves	1 tablespoon
Flour	3 tablespoons
Mace	1 tablespoon
Butter	3 tablespoons
Water	as needed
Bacon Grease	

Place water in pot and bring to boil. Place buffalo tongue in boiling water and allow to boil for fifteen minutes. Dice and sauté an onion in bacon grease. When the buffalo tongue is completely boiled split it and place cloves in the split(s). The tongue should then be covered with powdered mace and flour. Place butter in a frying pan and melt. Add sautéed onions and tongue to pan and allow to brown over low coals. Serve hot.

Note: Buffalo tongue was considered a 19th century delicacy. Many of the tongues which made it to the great restaurants of the East were smoked or pickled. Emigrants would have the opportunity to eat fresh tongues. Many find the tastebuds...well... distasteful. (That's an oxymoron... right?) The taste buds are rough, like those on a cat. If you don't like the texture... just cut them off.

Elk Roast

Elk Roast	roughly 2-4 pounds
Flour	3/4 cup
Onions	2
Carrots	3
Garlic	1 clove
Irish Potatoes	4 pounds
Celery	1/4 cup
Peppercorns	1/2 teaspoon
Salt	1/2 teaspoon
Rosemary	1/4 teaspoon
Sweet Basil	1/4 teaspoon
Water	2 quarts
Brandy	1 cup

Marinate the elk roast in brandy for one hour. Pound flour into the elk meat. Place floured roast in large pot and add water. Place over medium coals and cover until water begins to boil. Dice onions, celery, and carrots and add to the pot. Once this is done reduce heat to a simmer. Quarter potatoes and add to pot. Add all spices and diced clove of garlic. Simmer in covered pot for from three to five hours. The longer the meat is allowed to simmer the more tender and flavorful it will become.

Note: Elk (Wapiti) would have been available on portions of the trip. The elk of the 19th century did not all inhabit only mountainous areas. Hunting and grazing pressures of the past hundred or more years have forced them almost exclusively to the high ground. Odds are that in 1846 the elk in the Great Western Desert often would have occupied well-watered lowlands and would have been available to hunters. Elk meat is quite flavorful without being "gamey."

Patty Melt

Ground Beef	2 pounds
Onion	1
Black Peppercorns	1/8 tablespoon
Garlic Salt	1/8 teaspoon
Worcestershire Sauce	1 teaspoon
Olive Oil	8 tablespoons
Sharp Cheddar Cheese	1/8 pound
Rosemary spears	a pinch
Rye Bread	½ loaf

Chop the onion fine and sauté to a golden brown in four Tbs. of olive oil.

In a bowl mix the onion, ground beef, crushed peppercorns, garlic salt, Worcestershire sauce, and rosemary spears until uniform. Shape the mixture into patties.

Warm a frying pan with four Tbs. of olive oil in it and add patties. Cook as desired but flipping the patties often, though a little crisping of the patties adds flavor.

Butter an appropriate number of slices of rye bread and lightly toast on a cast-iron griddle. Slice or shred the cheese. When one side of a slice is toasted butter the uncooked side and flip the slice. Pile on cheese and put a patty on the cheese to aid with melting. When the second side of the slices are toasted the dish is ready. Serve hot and have your answer ready when asked for seconds.

Petite Chicken Pie

Chicken	2 pounds
Corn	3 cups, removed from cob
Onion	1
Carrot	1
Eggs	3
Milk	3 cups
Butter	7 tablespoons
Salt	2 teaspoons
Peppercorns	1 teaspoon, crushed

The chicken should be washed and cut into stew-size pieces. Place the chicken in a pot with a diced onion and water (three cups). Place over hot coals and boil for one hour. While this is going on make a crust as follows. Sift flour and add ½ teaspoon of salt in a bowl. To this add butter (five tablespoons), one egg and a little water (just a few tablespoons). Roll out the dough on a floured board and use to line the bottom of a deep pie pan or Dutch oven. Boil the corn for fifteen minutes and set aside to cool. Mix the remaining eggs with the milk and corn. Add the chicken and the onion to the bottom of the pie pan/Dutch oven. Pour in the milk/egg/corn mixture. Slice the carrot and add to the top of the mixture. Add remaining butter, salt, and peppercorns. Cover the pan/Dutch oven with another piece of crust and seal. Cut large slash across top of pie. Cook in a moderate oven or over moderate coals (be sure to cover in this instance). Cooking will take thirty to forty minutes. One may wish to use some of the broth produced by boiling the chicken and onion to wet the top crust during cooking to prevent burning.

Travelers often kept chickens with them to provide eggs. Some of these would be consumed along the way. Once a good layer stops producing, it's time for the main course. Additionally the plains were rich with prairie chickens or sage hens, which made for a welcome change in the diet of buffalo or antelope. Sage hen really doesn't taste like chicken. The meat has a different texture but is flavorful when cooked properly.

Grand Chicken Pie
(A good dish is worth having two recipes)

Chickens	3
Onions	2
Celery	1/4 cup
Mace	2 tablespoons
Sausage	1/4 pound
Ham	1/4 pound
Eggs	hard-boiled - 3
	uncooked yolk - 1
Peppercorns	1 tablespoon
Salt	2 tablespoons
Nutmeg	1 teaspoon

Cut up three small chickens and place all meat except the giblets, neck and drumsticks in a stew pot. Add diced onions, celery, and mace. Stew over medium coals for approximately one hour. Line a large Dutch oven with your favorite pie crust or puff pastry. To this add slices of ham, slices of sausage, sliced eggs, and the contents of the stew pot save the liquor. Add crushed peppercorns, salt, and nutmeg. Take one cup of the stew pot liquor and add to the pie. Cover with pie crust or puff paste. Glaze the top with the beaten yolk of an egg. Bake over low coals for 1 to 1 1/2 hours. Be sure to keep the heat as even as possible.

This dish may be served either hot or cold. Some may wish to add their favorite soup greens (such as spinach, etc.) to the pie.

Note: Some of the meat pies took on gargantuan proportions. This dish will easily serve a family of four. So when those hens stop laying, fear not, they still can contribute to the family meal.

Slovenly Josephs

This dish is included as a special request to a fan of the first edition, though that request was for something referred to as "Sloppy Joes." The dish makes good use of leftovers, a theme at the core of the Donner Party story, to make a hearty meal. Two versions are included here. Both use the elk roast and basic bread recipes in this book. One uses the delicious walnut catsup recipe. If you don't have elk, the recipe works well with chopped beef roast or even ground beef. If you don't have the walnut catsup any catsup from the mercantile will do in a pinch. The beauty of using the walnut catsup lies in its ability to stain all the porous materials it encounters, adding truth to the slovenly sobriquet.

Elk roast meat	1-2 pounds cooked
Rosemary spears	1/4 teaspoon
Garlic	1/2 clove
Peppercorns	1/2 teaspoon
Onion	1
Olive oil	as necessary
Tomatoes	6 counces pureed
Pepper sauce	to taste
Water	as necessary

Chop onion fine and sauté in olive oil until caramelized. Chop the elk meat very fine and add to caramelized onion.
Stir in pureed tomato. Crush garlic and peppercorns and add to mixture. Add rosemary spears and pepper sauce while the mixture simmers over a low flame. Simmer for twenty minutes, stirring mixture so it does not scorch. If the mixture begins to thicken too much stir in water as needed.

Serve hot by pouring mixture on thick slabs of the basic bread. The more adventurous might wish to top the dish with shredded cheese.

Unkempt Josephs

Elk roast meat	1 1/2 pounds cooked
Onion	3/4 cup chopped
Flour	2 Tablespoons
Water	3/4 cup
Walnut catsup	1 cup (can use regular catsup)
Worcestershire sauce	1 Tablespoon
Brown sugar	2 Tablespoons
Salt	to taste
Pepper	to taste

Add meat and onion to a frying pan and complete the browning of the meat. Add in flour, water, catsup, Worcestershire sauce, brown sugar, salt and pepper. Stir the mixture well and simmer for one-half hour at a minimum.

Serve hot over basic bread or buns.

(Courtesy of Penny Vyvey Walters)

Hash

Meat	one pound
Onions	4
Potatoes	4
Milk	1 cup
Butter	4 tablespoons
Salt	1 tablespoon
Peppercorns	1 tablespoon, crushed
Water	As needed

Slice potatoes, dice onions, and chop meat fine. Mix together in pot and add a few tablespoons of water (sufficient to allow boiling). Cover pot and place over moderate to high coals and cook until the whole is cooked completely. In the final few minutes of cooking add milk, butter, salt, and peppercorns. Stir until the mixture has an even consistency. Serve hot.

Those who wish to spice up this mixture can add ginger root or pepper sauce to taste.

Note: This recipe works for a variety of meats including mutton, beef, pork, buffalo, antelope, moose, elk, venison, horse, dog, prairie dog, sage hen, etc. Hash is often served to make a flavorful treat out of some of the less palatable cuts of meat. Good cuts of meat improve the overall product.

Jerked Meat

Meat
Salt

This process works best on lean meat from buffalo, moose, deer, antelope, elk, or sheep. Fatty meats such as bear, beef, pork, etc. will require additional drying time. Take meat and cut into long, thin strips. Rub salt into the meat and hang in the sun for several days until dried. The process can be shortened considerably by hanging the meat over a low, smokey fire. The latter process would allow one to dry meat in four to six hours.

Other flavorings, such as peppercorns and mustard seeds, can be added to the meat.

Note: A fair amount of the meat gathered by emigrants was dried and converted to "jerky." Since the slow process of hanging the meat in the sun could take days it is likely that most emigrants dried meat over the fire.

Basic Bread

Flour	4 cups
Scalded Milk/Water	at least 1 1/2 cups
Lard	2 tablespoons
Loaf Sugar	3 tablespoons
Salt	2 teaspoons
Yeast/Leavening	1 tablespoon

Dissolve yeast, salt, lard, and sugar in bowl of warm milk/water. Add flour and knead until a smooth dough results. If the dough is too stiff add more milk/water until desired consistency is attained. If the dough is too runny add more flour until desired consistency is attained. Knead the dough for roughly fifteen minutes after it has reached the desired consistency. Place in a greased pan and cover with a cloth. Place the pan in a warm place but not over or too near a heat source. Let rise for roughly one hour or until the loaf has reached the desired size. Bake in a moderate oven or in a dutch oven over moderate coals (no more than 400 degrees) for 30-45 minutes. When the bread is baked it will produce a hollow sound when tapped with a finger.

Note: No kitchen is complete without a basic bread recipe. This one reflects our ancestors' predilection to having a very rich bread. Most bread on the trail probably was made in a Dutch oven. Remember if you are using one of these to put coals both above (on the lid) and below the oven for more even baking.

Hard Bread, Hardtack, Biscuit, Sea Biscuit, Hard Crackers, Pilot Bread

Flour	6 cups
Milk/Water	as necessary
Lard	1/2 cup
Salt	2 Tablespoons
Raw/Brown Sugar	4 Tablespoons

Melt lard and mix with flour, sugar, and salt. Add milk/water to the mixture sufficient to make a stiff dough. Roll dough on floured board to 1/2 inch in thickness. Cut into squares approximately three inches on a side. Perforate roughly ten holes into the squares with a nail (this promotes drying).

Bake in an oven on a greased cookie sheet. The oven should be kept at a low temperature and the biscuits should be checked frequently to avoid burning. Turn biscuits on the sheet every ten minutes or so. Depending on temperature, dough consistency, and altitude, bake for anywhere from 30 to 90 minutes. Biscuits will turn a golden brown and will become extremely hard. Some say good hard tack will deflect a bullet but this is likely an exaggeration. When properly baked hard tack can last without spoilage for years.

For more flavorful hard bread one can add any handy extract (vanilla, lemon, orange, etc.) to taste when preparing the dough. Scalded milk and or soured milk can also be used. Hard biscuits can also be made over a campfire using a dutch oven.

Note: The average emigrant carried many pounds of pre-made biscuit on the trek with them. It is difficult to find appropriately made biscuit these days. This recipe will allow you to make your own hard bread.

Hard bread was used as an ingredient in many other dishes. This was the survival food which sustained many emigrants to their destination. In a pinch hard bread can be pulverized and used as flour for other recipes. Breaking pieces of hard bread into bite-sized fragments and adding these to a stew turns the hard bread into wonderful dumplings.

Examples of hard bread made in the 1860s are equally edible now as when they were made. How edible that is remains a point of contention. The hard biscuits often have the same effects as Journeycakes on the constitution.

Rice Bread

Rice	1 cup
Rice Flour	8 cups
Water/Milk	as necessary
Yeast	1 tablespoon
Brown Sugar	2 tablespoons

Boil rice until thoroughly cooked and soft. Add sugar, yeast, and rice flour. Knead until a smooth dough is formed, adding water/milk as necessary. Allow to rise in a warm place for roughly one hour. Shape into a large loaf or two small loaves. Allow to rise in baking vessel 1/2 hour. Place in moderate oven (or dutch oven over moderate coals no greater than 400 degrees in temperature) until baked (usually 30-45 minutes). When fully baked the loaves will give a hollow sound when tapped with a finger.

Note: Rice bread was a popular substitute for wheat bread. It is different but quite flavorful.

Corn Bread

Indian (Corn) Meal	2 cups
Milk	1 Pint
Eggs	3
Salt	1 teaspoon
Butter/Lard	2 tablespoons

Scald the milk and add corn meal. Mix in eggs, melted butter, and salt. Place is a greased cake pan or greased Dutch oven. Cook in a moderate oven or over moderate coals for 45 minutes to one hour.

Another Recipe:

Indian (Corn) Meal	1 cup
Flour	1 cup
Baking Powder	4 teaspoons
Egg	1
Milk	1 cup
Lard or Bacon Grease	1/4 cup
Loaf Sugar	"a pinch"
Salt	1/2 teaspoon

Beat an egg and mix with milk and melted lard/bacon grease in a pan. When the liquid is well-mixed add salt and baking powder. Stir in corn meal. and then flour. Cook in a moderate oven for 40 to 50 minutes.

Note: Corn bread is a favorite soft bread. Corn bread is exceptional for lapping up hot bacon grease. Many period recipes still refer to corn meal as "Indian meal."

Cinnamon Loaf

Flour	5 cups
Scalded Milk/Water	at least 1 1/2 cups
Lard	2 tablespoons
Butter	8 tablespoons
Loaf Sugar	4 tablespoons
Salt	2 teaspoons
Yeast/Leavening	1 tablespoon
Cinnamon	5 tablespoons
Confectioner's Sugar	9 tablespoons

Dissolve yeast, salt, lard, and three tablespoons of loaf sugar in bowl of warm milk/water. Add in flour and knead until a smooth dough results. If the dough is too stiff add more milk/water until desired consistency is attained. If the dough is too runny add more flour until desired consistency is attained. Knead the dough for roughly fifteen minutes after it has reached the desired consistency.

Roll the dough out thin and butter the top. Mix cinnamon with one tablespoon of loaf sugar. Sprinkle this mixture on the buttered dough and roll into a loaf.

Place the rolled loaf in a greased pan and cover with a cloth. Place the pan in a warm place but not over or too near a heat source. Let rise for roughly one hour or until the loaf has reached the desired size. Bake in a moderate oven or in a dutch oven over moderate coals (no more than 400 degrees) for between thirty and forty-five minutes. When the bread is baked it will produce a hollow sound when tapped with a finger.

When bread is cool make a frosting of six tablespoons of hot lard mixed with confectioner's sugar. Coat top of loaf with the frosting.

Some may wish to substitute butter for lard when making the frosting. The frosting can be made more flavorful by adding any kind of extract.

Note: This recipe makes a fine holiday bread or bread for any special occasion.

Pound Cake

Flour   2 ½ cups
Eggs   6
Butter   1 cup
Loaf Sugar   3/4 cup
Mace   1/2 tablespoon

Melt butter and add eggs in a bowl. Stir in flour, sugar, and mace until a smooth batter results. If the batter is too thick it can be thinned with additional eggs or milk. Place in a greased baking pan or Dutch oven and cook (covered) over medium coals for 45 minutes to one hour.

Note: This recipe produces a very rich cake. In many regards this is typical of 19th century baking, which has many heavy recipes. No, it doesn't weigh a pound!

Crumb Cake

Bread Crumbs	4 cups
Flour	1/2 cup
Soured Milk	1 cup
Water	As needed
Sugar	1 tablespoon
Eggs	1
Salt	1 teaspoon

Save up bread crumbs and crusts from the table. If you haven't saved up crumbs then use pulverized squares of hardtack. (Place the hardtack in a scarf and place on an anvil, such as a rock or wagon wheel. Pound the scarf until the hard bread is completely broken apart.) When crumb cakes are desired mix the crumbs with flour, salt, one egg, and soured milk. Add water until the batter is very smooth. Cook in bacon grease, butter, or lard over low coals.

Adventurous palates might wish to add cinnamon, nutmeg, and cloves to the batter.

Note: Just because the emigrants were traveling far from civilization did not mean that they lost their taste for sweets. This is a recipe which allows one to indulge a sweet tooth while using materials which are likely to be on hand during the journey.

The hint regarding substituting hard bread for crumbs can be used in a variety of recipes suggested here which call for flour.

Baked Apples

Apples   1 peck
Loaf Sugar
Cinnamon
Water

Peel all apples and removed any bruises. The apples should then be cored. Mix sugar and cinnamon together (five parts sugar to one part cinnamon). Insert the sugar/cinnamon mixture into the core holes. Place in the bottom of a Dutch oven which has a small quantity of water in it. Cover and bake over low coals until brown. Serve hot or cold.

Note: Odds are that most of the apples consumed by emigrants heading west were dried. However, eastward traveling emigrants might have been able to procure apples in Utah once the Mormon orchards were operative. The above recipe can be used for pears as well.

Ginger Cakes

Ginger cakes are a variation on a favorite dating back to the colonization of the Americas. Ginger has long been recognized as having properties that fight nausea. What a devilishly clever idea to create a dish that can both make one nauseous while preventing nausea! It really is a strange world.

Ginger root	2+ tablespoons (ground)
Nutmeg	½ teaspoon (ground)
Scalded milk or cream	2 cups
Butter	4 tablespoons
Eggs	2
Flour	7+ cups
Sugar	1 1/4 cups
Baking soda	1 ½ tablespoons

To the scalded milk or warm cream add the butter and eggs, stirring until the mixture is consistent. (I find the cream a little rich but it does produce wonderful results.) Next stir in the sugar, nutmeg, and ginger until the mixture is once again consistent. The quantity of ginger depends upon the potency of the ginger root and the amount of bite desired in the cakes. Add the baking soda and flour and knead until the bread stiffens. Larger eggs may require the use of more flour. The dough should be rolled thin and the cakes can be shaped by pressing a tin cup into the mixture, though one can use a knife to whittle any shape which pleases the imagination. One can even place the entire mixture in a cake pan and cook it as a single cake (requires more baking time). Bake in a moderate oven for roughly 10-15 minutes. Bake until the cakes retain some softness but are not too rubbery. If the temperature gets away from you just call them ginger snaps and let the kids have them.

(I once mistakenly added buckwheat flour to the other ingredients with interesting results. The cakes did not rise so well and were substantially heavier. However, they were quite palatable with warm milk poured over them.)

Ladyfingers

Forget those sponge cake dainties we presently call "ladyfingers." In the 19th Century ladyfingers were sufficiently rich to be whet the most voracious of appetites. Start with the basic bread dough recipe from this book. If the ladyfingers are to be deep fried in grease then you can omit putting yeast in the dough. If you choose to bake the ladyfingers, the yeast goes in. Roll the dough very thin and cut into rectangles, five inches by two inches.

Dice the intended stuffing for the ladyfingers. A wide variety of fillings work well. My favorites are a combination of cheeses and spiced meats (try the minced meat recipe or the scrapple for this). However, one can put in cheese with sautéed onions, mushrooms, etc. For a more modern flair put in some pizza sauce, cheese, and other normal pizza toppings. For naughtier fingers one can put various peppers into the dough mix. I like red chili peppers in such a role.

Place the stuffing on the dough strips and roll them all together into a finger shape. The dough becomes a tube which is filled with the selected goodies. Be sure to pinch off the ends of the tube. The tube can then be dropped for a few moments into hot grease or be baked in a moderate oven until the outside browns. Serve hot or cold. Your guests will appreciate getting the finger on this occasion.

Coffee

Coffee Beans	1 pint
Egg	1
Water	1 gallon
Loaf Sugar	to taste
Milk	to taste

Carefully roast the beans in a tin cup over moderate coals. Be sure to swirl the cup to assure uniform roasting. Be careful of the coffee oil as it is highly flammable. Once the beans are sufficiently roasted they can be crushed with a hammer or pestle. If a grinder is available, they can be ground.

Heat the water in a large kettle or coffee pot. Add the crushed/ground coffee and boil for fifteen to twenty minutes. Remove from the coals and stir in the egg for additional richness and clarity. Skim the crushed beans and reuse as necessary.

Milk and sugar commonly are added.

Note: We often wonder about the incredible abilities of our pioneer ancestors to endure week upon week of hard, back-breaking labor. Some of it might have related to the intensive consumption of coffee, which was common in the 19th century. Lets face it... most of our ancestors were wired on caffeine (among other things)! A military issue to a soldier of the period would be roughly one pint of coffee beans per day, enough to make at least two gallons of very strong coffee and another one or two of moderately strong coffee. Many of our ancestors actually chewed the coffee beans while they worked.

Those who could afford coffee and had no religious restrictions on the beverage tended to consume a lot of coffee. This practice had unforseen advantages to the emigrants. The big killer of emigrants was cholera, caused by drinking tainted water. Any individuals who consumed coffee (and teas) boiled the water first and lessened their chances of contracting water-bourne diseases.

Carrot Coffee

Carrots   3 cups
Water   1 gallon

The carrots should be sliced thin and dried slowly in an oven or near (but not over) the fire. Once they are dried they store well and can be kept without spoilage for months.

Heat water to a boil in a large kettle. Add dried carrots and allow to boil for twenty minutes. Skim off the carrots and eat them. Serve carrot coffee piping hot.

Note: Many emigrants did not pack sufficient luxury foodstuffs, like coffee beans, for the entire journey. When the coffee was gone it was difficult (and expensive) to find on the trail. Accordingly many had to improvise substitute hot beverages. Carrot coffee is but one of many substitutes, such a Mormon tea (ephedra), which was used. Carrot coffee will not get you wired, but certainly will fulfill that desire to have a flavorful hot drink. I personally like to put a dash of beef tallow in the coffee to give it a beef broth flavor.

Why don't he write?

Planning Your Own Donner Party

So you want to ~~inflict~~ try out some of the wonderful recipes above on your friends and family? Unless you've got a really tolerant group at your office potluck you may need to go to the extreme of throwing your own Donner Party. You can always claim that you were attempting to throw a "Dinner Party" and the automatic spelling correction let you down. However, anyone who works with such programs will find just the opposite and most will attempt to correct "Donner Party" to "Dinner Party." There's something disturbing in this.

Don't panic. It's really very easy to throw a Donner Party. You don't need wagons...though that would be a nice touch. You don't need starving people...though that might help many get over some modern prejudices against eating the rich foods of our ancestors. Here are the basic ingredients you need.

Timing

Let's face it, the Donner theme cries for a winter feast. Doesn't it just feel out of place to put up Christmas decorations during the summer? Well, it should feel the same to plan a Donner Party in June. A cold February day is recommended. If you're one of those unfortunates who lives in a place where there is no real winter then turn up the air conditioning...have fake snow brought in...or travel north. What better place to throw a party than at a Chalet in the mountains?

I've been in Phoenix when it has been snowing. When offered such a gift from the skies, instead of sitting there waiting for the city's one snow plow to get to your block call up your friends and have an impromptu Donner Party. In other words work with what Mother Nature gives you.

If Mother Nature does not support your party efforts, go around her. Bring in blocks of ice. Have a local ice sculptor carve a covered wagon. Rent out a large meat locker as the venue for the party. Take the party to a ski resort, where they make snow for most of the year. Go to a mountain top and party atop a glacier.

Setting

Once you've got the winter thing worked out, you want to work out the perfect setting for your event. Of course, the perfect setting would be at the Donner campsites near Donner Lake. Few will have the resources and courage to go face the ghosts. So the average Donner Party will probably be held closer to your home. Good Donner parties are outdoor events. A secluded mountain place is an excellent location. Just remember the **Donners were snowshoers and hikers. They did not cross-county ski or snowmobile!** (Oops... I digress.) A public park can suit your purposes. Somehow... the beach probably will not work. Scantily clad people in period hats playing beach volleyball does not seem to hit the heart of the theme we're trying to establish here. But, it is your party, make the best of it.

Most will opt to have their Donner Party in their very own back yard or even on the patio. At this point a thought might have occurred to you as to how the setting and the timing combine. Wait a second... a winter, outdoor party? That's right! We've become spoiled. During the winter few of us consider the wonderful flavor which barbecued meat has. Come summer though...we're out in the back yard cooking away. Get into the real world...you can actually cook outdoors in the winter. Barbequing a steak when it's forty degrees below zero is a bit more challenging than doing it during the dog days of summer. However, it can be done. Just keep flipping the meat to keep the top warm and eat very fast.

Foods

The recipe section of this book has provided several dishes that are especially suited to your party. I recommend making "Donner Stew" using the stew recipe. This dish is easy to keep warm, simple to make, and provides the most mileage for off-color jokes. You can tell your guests that it contains "mystery meat" or you used "whatever was lying around the kitchen." For special effects don't forget to go to the butcher and get some bones to throw in the pot.

No doubt most Donner Parties will include 21st century foods as well. Potato chips and cheese twists will likely arrive with the guests if you don't provide them. Go with the flow and live with it. Avocado dip happens! If it's cold enough these dishes will lose their appeal. Imagine trying to dip a corn chip in frozen guacamole. Frozen cheese puffs are just wrong. Frozen marshmallows will be almost impossible to chew. Nature will take care of the junk food.

Something to remember is that the Donner Party didn't have a lot of alcoholic beverages on hand, at least not after the glorious Indpendence Day clebration. Bringing a keg would not appear to be appropriate. But heck, if the keg shows up, it must be the will of higher powers. If you want to risk having your guests get sick on the combination of buffalo tongue, brain stew, and beer... go for it. I'm just glad I don't have to clean up things.

Your guests have asked, "What can we bring?" Do you respond, "nothing?" No! Here's where you get them to try their hands at 19th century cooking. Pick out one of the exciting recipes, say... Buffalo tongue or gruel, and have them bring that. One can make the dish selection fun by running it as a lottery and having your guest pick the recipe page out of a period hat or bonnet. There most likely will be an extended silence when you tell them what you want. But if they're really good friends, they'll get into the spirit of the thing and play along. They may actually find that they want to learn more about good, old-fashioned cooking.

Once you have the menu worked out you will need to consider the amount of food you wish to serve. An authentic experience would call for scrupulously small portions. However, IT'S A PARTY. Loosen up and have fun! It's ok to have enough food to choke all your guests. Just don't really choke any of them and keep in mind that the cold will reduce the bad effects of too many calories by forcing the body to burn them faster, even when doing something as restful as conversing.

Decorations

So how does one decorate for a Donner Party? Snowdrifts, a wagon, and a canvas tent are great touches. The more macabre hosts might wish to have the snowdrifts festooned with mannequin parts, such as arms and legs. A small fire with a simmering pot of stew hanging above from a tripod is a wonderful effect and could keep some of the snacks warm enough to eat. If you're holding your party indoors, try hanging canvas in the living room to give it the feeling of the interior of a tent.

Costumes

Believe it or not there are dozens of clothing manufacturers who make mid-nineteenth century clothing. The completely authentic look from head to toe will likely cost several hundred dollars, unless one is a talented tailor or seamstress. For those who can't afford detailed costumes, a beat-up period looking hat or bonnet and wrapping oneself in an old wool blanket or quilt can provide an appropriate effect.

No, a dance-hall girl outfit does not fit the occasion no matter how attractive those costumes look. Instead one should go for the plain pioneer woman look. Similarly showing up with a butcher's template for the various cuts of meat upon one's skin, while humorous, is in questionable taste. Mountain man buckskins are also out of place, unless one wishes to try boiling some of the buckskin as the Donners would have done.

Entertainment

There are lots of interesting entertainments one can use. If the party is outdoors there are a variety of winter sports that might be fun. Snowshoe races can be amusing...especially with participants who have never snowshoed before. A trick I learned by snowshoeing with my dogs is that if anyone steps on the end of the snowshoe, the snowshoer is stuck. Once my dogs figured this out they found it very amusing to apply the brakes at inoportune times and, no doubt, people will have similar satisfaction.

Snowball fights and building snow people, or parts thereof, can also be part of the party. Perhaps bobbing for stew meat or potatoes in a tub of water just cold enough to have a thin skin of ice on the surface is appropriate for an extreme experience. I guarantee that if you manage to get your face through the ice and plunge the entire head into the water, you'll feel just about every hair follicle on your head.

If one has access to buffalo chips this opens a variety of activities including a chip throwing contest, a chip gathering contest, and one to cook over a chip fire. Of course, this increases the chances that the party will be remembered as being crappy, but it will be memorable.

Of course, keeping your food warm on a period tin plate, while the cold wind is whistling through the party will have a unique entertainment value of its own. Have your guests with musical inclinations bring instruments and entertain the group. Of course the fine art of conversation is most appropriate.

If your party is indoors you have a variety of entertaining activities which might be fun. These can range from bobbing for potatoes to drawing cards to see who gets to eat which delicious dish. One might wish to take a bag of coins and hide them somewhere in the home. Scavenger hunts are appropriate.

For the more technically inclined, one can show the Ric Burns' PBS special called *The Donner Party* or even Trey Parker's *Cannibal: The Musical*. The former is far more educational and will help set the tone for the party. The musical relates to a later famous episode of cannibalism but is very funny. There are plenty of B movies with a Donner Party theme as well that are sure to fit in with the party.

Advertising Your Party

Attached are sample posters for advertising your party. Just remember to emphasize that "It's a Donner Party... not a Dahmer Party!" Jeffrey Dahmer was known as the Milwaukee Cannibal. The similarity in sound and subject matter often creates some confusion, especially the closer one gets to Milwaukee. If your guests can't get past the similarities, just call out "It's Miller Time" and go on with the festivities. By the way, if you are a restaurateur, mortician, or doctor it is seriously recommended that for your career's sake you not throw a Donner party at all. Remember if you are using a spell-checker on your invitations, you might pay attention that the word processor program might change "Donner" to "Dinner." I don't think it is anything intentional. However, some of those software designers have a strange sense of humor.

In closing remember that it is better to be a party animal than be on the menu. Have fun and be the party!

You are Cordially Invited to a Donner Party!
Lose Weight and Celebrate All at the Same Time!

Time:

Place:

Dress: Historical Attire Preferred
(This will be an outdoor party so dress accordingly.)

This is a theme party based on the mid-nineteenth Century wagon company that became stranded in the Mountains and were forced to become cannibals to survive the winter.

Please bring a dish appropriate to the period.
Call me if you want ideas!
R.S.V.P.

Pot Mis-fortune Dinner!
A Donner Party!!!!!!!

Time:

Place:

Dress: Historical Attire Preferred

(This will be an outdoor party so dress accordingly.) There will be a scavenger hunt. This is a theme party based on the mid-nineteenth Century wagon company that became stranded in the Sierra Nevada Mountains and were forced to become cannibals to survive the winter.

Please bring a dish appropriate to the period. Call me if you want ideas!

People are dying to attend so R.S.V.P.

Are You Done With Those Ladyfingers?
Leftovers Are Lifesavers!
You are Cordially Invited
to a Donner/Dinner Party!

In the tradition of the Donner Party, America's most famous cannibals, we are commemorating the events of 1846-1847 with a Donner/Dinner Party. Brings whatever leftovers you have or whatever's lying around and we will figure out what to do with it from there. Period costumes and ravenous appetites are recommended.

No clown food please as cannibals say, "Clowns taste funny."

R.S.V.P.

Bibliography

There are a host of previously published works on the Donner Party, many penned by survivors of the ordeal. Writings such as the *History of the Donner Party* by C.F. McGlashan and *Ordeal by Hunger* by G.R. Stewart are perennial favorites and provide useful starting points for the study of the Donner Party. More recent works such as *Unfortunate Emigrants* by Kristin Johnson, *Overland Diaries in 1846* by D. Morgan, and *West From Fort Bridger* by J.R. Korns and D. Morgan pull together important sources and are exceptionally useful. The preparation for this book draws upon many such publications. Those readers wishing to know more about these emigrants and their fate are directed to these sources and the references below for a combination of scholarly and first-hand treatments of the subject matter. There is a wealth of excellent research to draw upon.

We all are indebted to the historians and participants whose efforts have preserved and disseminated these words for us to ponder. Without such a wealth of information the richness of the struggles and the breadth of human emotions would be lost.

Selected References:

Breen, Patrick. 1910, Diary of Patrick Breen: One of the Donner Party. *Publications of the Academy of Pacific Coast History* 1:6.

Bryant, E. 1848, *What I Saw in California*. New York, D. Appleton.

DeVoto, B. 1943, *The Year of Decision 1846*. Boston, Little, Brown and Company.

Farnham, Eliza W. 1856, *California In-Doors and Out*. New York, Dix Edwards.

Graves, William C. 1877, Crossing the Plains in '46. Published in four installments (April-May) in the *Russian River Flag*.

Hardesty, D.L. 1997, *The Archaeology of the Donner Party*. Reno, University of Nevada Press.

Harlan, J.W. 1888, *California '46 to '88*. San Francisco, Bancroft.

Hastings, L.W. 1845, *The Emigrants' Guide to Oregon and California*.

Hawkins, B.R. and D.B. Madsen. 1990, *Excavation of the Donner-Reed Wagons: Historic Archaeology Along the Hastings Cutoff*. Salt Lake City, University of Utah Press.

Houghton, E.P. Donner. 1911, *The Expedition of the Donner Party and Its Tragic Fate*. Chicago, A.C. McClurg & Co.

King, J.A. 1992, *Winter of Entrapment a New Look at the Donner Party*. Toronto, P.D. Meany Publishers.

Korns, J. Roderic (ed. by D. Morgan). 1951, West from Fort Bridger. *Utah Historical Quarterly* 19. (Reprinted with revisions and updates by W. Bagley and H. Schindler in 1994 through Utah State University Press).

Lavender, D. 1996, *Snowbound the Tragic Story of the Donner Party*. New York, Holiday House.

Limburg, P.R. 1998, *Deceived the Story of the Donner Party*. Pacifica, International Publishing Services.

McGlahsan, C.F. 1880, *History of the Donner Party a Tragedy of the Sierra*. San Francisco, A.L. Bancroft Company.

McLaughlin, Mark. 2007, *The Donner Party: Weathering the Storm*. Carneilian Bay, Mic Mac Publishing.

Morgan, D. 1943, *The Humboldt Highland of the West*. New York, Farrar and Reinhardt.

Morgan, D. 1963, *Overland in 1846: Diaries and Letters of the California-Oregon Trail*. Georgetown, Talisman Press.

Mullen, F. Jr. 1997, *The Donner Party Chronicles*. Halcyon Imprint for the Nevada Humanities Committee.

Stewart, G.R. 1960, *Ordeal by Hunger the Story of the Donner Party*. Boston, Houghton-Mifflin.

Stewart, G.R. 1962, *The California Trail*. Lincoln, University of Nebraska Press.

Stookey, W.M. 1950, *Fatal Decision the Tragic Story of the Donner Party*. Salt Lake City, Deseret Book Company.

Thornton, J.Q. 1996, *Camp of Death: The Donner Party Mountain Camp 1846-47*. Silverthorne, Vista Books.

Map:

The map presented in this book is a composite of a variety of sources. In 1846 the topography of the California Route was not well-known. For example, an 1846 map published by S. Augustus Mitchell shows a blank area for the land west of the Great Salt Lake until the Sierra Nevada mountains. In order to preserve a 19th century feel to the map it was decided to use the physiography as known in the 1860s supplemented by other maps.

Territory and Military Department of Utah compiled in the Bureau of Topographic Engineers of the War Department chiefly for military purposes under the authority of Honorable J.B. Floyd, Secretary of War, 1860. *Official Records of the War of the Rebellion*, Plate CXX. (This map was based on observations made by Captains Simpson and Macomb. It was modified in 1862 and published in 1891.)

Participants of the Donner Party

THE SURVIVORS

Edward Breen
Isabella Breen
James Breen
John Breen
Margaret Breen
Patrick Breen
Patrick Breen, Jr.
Peter Breen
Simon Breen
Elitha Donner
Eliza Donner
Frances Donner
George Donner II
Georgia Donner
Leanna Donner
Mary Donner
William Eddy
Sarah Graves Fosdick
Sarah Murphy Foster
William Foster
Eleanor Graves
Elizabeth Graves
Jonathan Graves
Lovinia Graves
Mary Graves
Nancy Graves
William Graves
Walter Herron
Solomon Hook
Noah James
Louis Keseberg
Phillipine Keseberg
Amanda McCutchen
William McCutchen
Hiram Miller
Mary Murphy
Simon Murphy
William Murphy
Harriet Murphy Pike

Naomi Pike
James F. Reed
James Reed, Jr.
Margaret Reed
Mary Jane "Patty" Reed
Thomas Reed
Virginia Reed
Thursday
Thursday's Friend
John Baptiste Trudeau
Eliza Williams
Dorothea Wolfinger

THE VICTIMS

Antonio
Charles Burger
John Denton
Patrick Dolan
Elizabeth Donner
George Donner
Isaac Donner
Jacob Donner
Lewis Donner
Samuel Donner
Tamsen Donner
Eleanor Eddy
James P. Eddy
Margaret Eddy
Milton Elliot
Jay Fosdick
George (Jeremiah) Foster
Elizabeth Graves, Sr.
Franklin Ward Graves, Sr.
Franklin Ward Graves, Jr.
Luis
Luke Halloran
Mr. Hardcoop
William Hook
Sarah Keyes

Ada Keseberg
Louis Keseberg, Jr.
Harriet McCutchen
John Landrum Murphy
Levinah Murphy
Lemuel Murphy
Catherine Pike
William Pike
Joseph Reinhardt
Salvador
Samuel Shoemaker
James Smith
Augustus Spitzer
Charles Stanton
John Synder
Bayliss Williams
Jacob Wolfinger

About the Author

Terry A. Del Bene holds a Doctorate in Anthropology and has participated in and organized living history programs throughout the United States. Since his retirement from a long career as an archaeologist Terry has focused his efforts on writing. He has also served as the Tribal Historic Preservation Officer for the Pit River Tribe in California.

Terry has authored and edited several books including *Echoes from the Bluffs 2, Images of America: Green River, Images of America: Grand Encampment, The Settlement of America,* and *'Dem Bon'z..*

www.ingramcontent.com/pod-product-compliance
Lightning Source LLC
Chambersburg PA
CBHW021151080526
44588CB00008B/291